COORDINATION GROUP PUBLICATIONS.

Organ-ise your Biology revision with CGP...

There's a lot to learn in Edexcel 9-1 International GCSE Biology, but CGP is here to take the stress out of your revision! We explain every topic with no-nonsense study notes, and there are plenty of practice questions to sharpen up your exam skills.

P.S. It's great for the Edexcel International GCSE Science Double Award too!

CGP — still the best! ☺

Our sole aim here at CGP is to produce the highest quality books — carefully written, immaculately presented and dangerously close to being funny.

Then we work our socks off to get them out to you
— at the cheapest possible prices.

Contents

Section 8 — Ecology and the Environment

Section 9 — Use of Biological Resources

Describing Experiments

Paper 2

Paper 2

This book covers both Biology Paper 1 and Biology
Paper 2 material. Some material is needed for Paper 2 only —
we've clearly marked this in green boxes.
The Paper 2 revision questions in the book are also printed in green.
If you're doing a Science (Double Award) qualification
you don't need to learn the Paper 2 material.

Published by CGP.

From original material by Paddy Gannon.

Editors: Sarah Armstrong, Katherine Faudemer and Emily Forsberg

ISBN: 978 1 78294 674 8

With thanks to Susan Alexander and Rachel Kordan for the proofreading.

With thanks to Jan Greenway for the copyright research.

Printed by Elanders Ltd, Newcastle upon Tyne.
Clipart from Corel®

Characteristics of Living Organisms

Welcome to the wonderful world of Biology. It's wonderful because it's all about you. Or at least, it's all about <u>living organisms</u> — which includes you. You may not think you have much in common with a slug or a mushroom, but you'd be wrong. You see, <u>all living organisms</u> share the same <u>eight basic characteristics</u>...

① They Need Nutrition

Living organisms need nutrients to provide them with <u>energy</u> and the <u>raw materials</u> for growth and repair. Nutrients include things like <u>proteins</u>, <u>fats</u> and <u>carbohydrates</u>, as well as <u>vitamins</u> and <u>minerals</u>. See pages 13 and 15.

② They Respire

Organisms <u>release energy</u> from their <u>food</u> by a process called <u>respiration</u>. See page 29.

③ They Excrete Their Waste

Waste products such as <u>carbon dioxide</u> and <u>urine</u> have to be <u>removed</u>. The removal of waste is called <u>excretion</u>. See page 42.

④ They Respond to Their Surroundings

Living organisms can <u>react</u> to <u>changes</u> in their <u>surroundings</u>. See page 45.

⑤ They Move

Organisms <u>move towards</u> things like <u>water</u> and <u>food</u>, and <u>away</u> from things like <u>predators</u> and <u>poisons</u>. Even plants can move a bit.

⑥ They Can Control Their Internal Conditions

Internal conditions include <u>temperature</u> and <u>water content</u>. See page 49.

⑦ They Reproduce

Organisms have to produce <u>offspring</u> (children) in order for their <u>species</u> to <u>survive</u>. See p.56-57.

⑧ They Grow and Develop

Yup, even the smallest organisms have to <u>grow</u> and <u>develop</u> into their <u>adult form</u>.

Hang on — that means Peter Pan wasn't a living organism...

Every single living thing shares these same eight characteristics. Amazing, huh? You'll be covering most of them in a lot more detail during the rest of your course, so if I were you, I'd commit them all to memory now.

Q1   What is the name of the process where waste is removed from an organism?   [1 mark]

Levels of Organisation

Living organisms are made up of <u>cells</u> — these are like <u>tiny building blocks</u>. Some organisms are <u>multicellular</u> — they contain <u>lots</u> of cells, which need some form of <u>organisation</u>. Some organisms consist of a <u>single cell</u>.

Cells Contain Organelles

1) Cells can be <u>eukaryotic</u> or <u>prokaryotic</u>. Eukaryotic cells are <u>complex</u>, and include all <u>animal</u> and <u>plant</u> cells. Prokaryotic cells are <u>smaller</u> and <u>simpler</u>, e.g. bacteria.

2) <u>Organelles</u> are tiny structures <u>within</u> cells. You can only see them using a powerful <u>microscope</u>.

3) Here are some of the organelles found in a <u>typical animal cell</u>:
   - <u>Nucleus</u>: an organelle which contains the <u>genetic material</u> that controls the cell's activities. It is surrounded by its <u>own membrane</u>.
   - <u>Cell membrane</u>: this membrane forms the <u>outer surface</u> of the cell and controls the substances that go <u>in</u> and <u>out</u>.
   - <u>Cytoplasm</u>: a gel-like substance where most of the cell's <u>chemical reactions</u> happen. It contains <u>enzymes</u> (see page 6) which control these reactions.
   - <u>Mitochondria</u> — small organelles where most of the reactions for <u>aerobic respiration</u> take place (see page 29). Respiration transfers energy that the cell needs to work.
   - <u>Ribosomes</u> — small organelles where <u>proteins</u> are made in the cell.

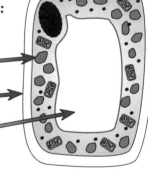

4) <u>Plant cells</u> usually have all the organelles that animal cells have, plus a <u>few extra</u>:
   - <u>Chloroplasts</u>: <u>photosynthesis</u>, which makes <u>food</u> for the plant (see p.20), happens here. Chloroplasts contain a green substance called <u>chlorophyll</u>, which is used in photosynthesis.
   - <u>Cell wall</u>: a rigid structure made of <u>cellulose</u>, which surrounds the cell membrane. It <u>supports</u> the cell and <u>strengthens</u> it.
   - <u>Vacuole</u>: a large organelle that contains <u>cell sap</u> (a weak solution of sugars and salts). It helps to <u>support</u> the cell.

Similar Cells are Organised into Tissues

1) A <u>tissue</u> is a group of similar cells that <u>work together</u> to carry out a <u>particular function</u>.
2) For example, plants have <u>xylem tissue</u> (for transporting water and mineral salts) and <u>phloem tissue</u> (for transporting sucrose and amino acids).
3) A tissue can contain <u>more than one</u> cell type (see next page).

These tissues have a very particular function...

Tissues are Organised into Organs

1) An <u>organ</u> is a group of different <u>tissues</u> that <u>work together</u> to perform a function.
2) <u>Lungs</u> in mammals and <u>leaves</u> on plants are two examples of <u>organs</u> — they're both made up of several <u>different tissue types</u>.

leaves

lungs

Organs Make Up Organ Systems

1) Organs work together to form <u>organ systems</u>. Each system does a <u>different job</u>.
2) For example, in mammals, the <u>digestive system</u> is made up of organs including the stomach, intestines, pancreas and liver.

Soft and quilted — the best kind of tissues...

Make sure you learn the features that plant and animal cells have in common as well as the differences between them.

Q1   Give two differences in structure between animal and plant cells.   [2 marks]

Specialised Cells and Stem Cells

Cells <u>don't</u> all look the <u>same</u>. They have <u>different structures</u> to suit their <u>different functions</u>.

Cells are Specialised

1) Most cells don't look exactly like the ones shown on the previous page. They're <u>specialised</u> to carry out a <u>particular function</u>, so their structures can vary.

2) For example, in humans, <u>red blood cells</u> are specialised for carrying oxygen and <u>white blood cells</u> are specialised for defending the body against disease.

red blood cells

white blood cell

Embryonic Stem Cells Can Turn into ANY Type of Cell

1) <u>Cell differentiation</u> is the process by which a cell <u>changes</u> to become <u>specialised</u> for its job.

2) As cells change, they develop <u>different organelles</u> and turn into <u>different types of cells</u>. This allows them to carry out <u>specific functions</u>.

3) <u>Undifferentiated</u> cells, called <u>stem cells</u>, can divide to produce lots <u>more</u> undifferentiated cells. They can differentiate into <u>different types of cell</u>, depending on what <u>instructions</u> they're given.

4) Stem cells are found in early <u>human embryos</u>. They're <u>exciting</u> to doctors and medical researchers because they have the potential to turn into <u>any</u> kind of cell at all. This makes sense if you think about it — <u>all</u> the <u>different types</u> of cell found in a human being have to come from those <u>few cells</u> in the early embryo.

5) Adults also have stem cells, but they're only found in certain places, like <u>bone marrow</u>. Unlike embryonic stem cells, they <u>can't</u> turn into <u>any</u> cell type at all, only certain ones, such as blood cells.

6) Stem cells from embryos and bone marrow can be grown in a lab to produce <u>clones</u> (<u>genetically identical cells</u>) and made to <u>differentiate</u> into specialised cells to use in <u>medicine</u> or <u>research</u>.

Stem Cells May Be Able to Cure Many Diseases

1) Medicine already uses <u>adult stem cells</u> to cure <u>disease</u>. For example, <u>stem cells</u> transferred from the bone marrow of a <u>healthy person</u> can <u>replace faulty blood cells</u> in the patient who receives them.

2) <u>Embryonic stem cells</u> could also be used to <u>replace faulty cells</u> in sick people — you could make <u>insulin-producing cells</u> for people with <u>diabetes</u>, <u>nerve cells</u> for people <u>paralysed by spinal injuries</u>, and so on.

3) However, there are <u>risks</u> involved in using stem cells in medicine. For example, stem cells grown in the lab may become <u>contaminated</u> with a <u>virus</u> which could be <u>passed on</u> to the patient and so make them <u>sicker</u>.

Some People Are Against Stem Cell Research

1) Some people are <u>against</u> stem cell research because they feel that human embryos <u>shouldn't</u> be used for experiments since each one is a <u>potential human life</u>.

2) Others think that curing existing patients who are <u>suffering</u> is more important than the rights of <u>embryos</u>.

3) One fairly convincing argument in favour of this point of view is that the embryos used in the research are usually <u>unwanted ones</u> from <u>fertility clinics</u> which, if they weren't used for research, would probably just be <u>destroyed</u>. But of course, campaigners for the rights of embryos usually want this banned too.

4) These campaigners feel that scientists should concentrate more on finding and developing <u>other sources</u> of stem cells, so people could be helped <u>without</u> having to use embryos.

But florists cell stems, and nobody complains about that...

Whatever your own opinion is, make sure you know some advantages and disadvantages of using stem cells.

Q1   Give one example of a specialised cell.   [1 mark]

Q2   Give one advantage and one disadvantage of using stem cells in medicine.   [2 marks]

Paper 2

Plants, Animals and Fungi

Living organisms can be arranged into groups, according to the features they have in common.
Three of these groups are plants, animals and fungi...

Learn the Features of Plants, Animals and Fungi

Plants, animals and fungi are eukaryotic organisms — they are made up of eukaryotic cells (see page 2). If you've ever wondered what features you share with a housefly, then this table is for you. Read on to find out more...

Plants, animals and fungi have different cell structures. For more on the structure of plant and animal cells, see page 2.

Organism		Description	Examples
Plants		1) Plants are multicellular. 2) They have chloroplasts (see p.2) which means they can photosynthesise (see p.20). 3) Their cells have cell walls, which are made of cellulose. 4) Plants store carbohydrates as sucrose or starch.	Flowering plants like: • cereals (e.g. maize). • herbaceous legumes (e.g. peas and beans).
Animals		1) Animals are also multicellular. 2) They don't have chloroplasts and they can't photosynthesise. 3) Their cells don't have cell walls. 4) Most have some kind of nervous coordination (see p.45). This means that they can respond rapidly to changes in their environment. 5) They can usually move around from one place to another. 6) They often store carbohydrate in the form of glycogen.	• Mammals (e.g. humans). • Insects (e.g. houseflies and mosquitoes).
Fungi		1) Some are single-celled. 2) Others have a body called a mycelium, which is made up of hyphae (thread-like structures). The hyphae contain lots of nuclei. 3) They can't photosynthesise. 4) Their cells have cell walls made of chitin. 5) Most feed by saprotrophic nutrition — they secrete extracellular enzymes into the area outside their body to dissolve their food, so they can then absorb the nutrients. 6) They can store carbohydrate as glycogen.	• Yeast — this is a single-celled fungus. • Mucor — this is multicellular and has a mycelium and hyphae.

I've avoided the classic 'he was a fungi to be with' joke...

OK, I'll admit it — that was a big chunk of information for you to get your head around. But if you learn the table above, you'll know everything you need to know about plants, animals and fungi. Excellent.

Q1   State the two ways that plants store carbohydrates.   [2 marks]

Q2   Give an example of a single-celled fungi.   [1 mark]

Protoctists, Bacteria and Viruses

Just when you thought you'd mastered all the groups — here's a few more you need to know about...

Learn the Features of Protoctists, Bacteria and Viruses

Protoctists are eukaryotic organisms (see p.4). Bacteria are prokaryotic organisms (single prokaryotic cells).

Organism		Description	Examples
Protoctists	nucleus	1) These are single-celled and microscopic (really tiny). 2) Some have chloroplasts and are similar to plant cells. 3) Others are more like animal cells.	• Chlorella (plant-cell-like) • Amoeba (animal-cell-like) — lives in pond water.
Bacteria	cell wall, cytoplasm, circular chromosome, cell membrane, plasmids (extra bits of DNA)	1) These are also single-celled and microscopic. 2) They don't have a nucleus. 3) They have a circular chromosome of DNA. 4) Some can photosynthesise. 5) Most bacteria feed off other organisms — both living and dead.	• Lactobacillus bulgaricus — can be used to make milk go sour and turn into yoghurt. It's rod-shaped. • Pneumococcus — spherical (round) in shape.
Viruses	protein coat, DNA or RNA. There's more on DNA on p.53. DNA and RNA are both nucleic acids, so they're fairly similar.	1) These are particles, rather than cells, and are smaller than bacteria. 2) They can only reproduce inside living cells. A virus is an example of a parasite — it depends on another organism to grow and reproduce. 3) They infect all types of living organisms. 4) They come in loads of different shapes and sizes. 5) They don't have a cellular structure — they have a protein coat around some genetic material (either DNA or RNA).	• Influenza virus • Tobacco mosaic virus — this makes the leaves of tobacco plants discoloured by stopping them from producing chloroplasts. • HIV

Some Organisms Are Pathogens

Pathogens are organisms that cause disease. They include some fungi, protoctists and bacteria. Viruses are also pathogens (even though they're not living organisms).

E.g.

PROTOCTIST: Plasmodium, which causes malaria.

BACTERIUM: Pneumococcus, which causes pneumonia.

VIRUSES: Influenza virus (which causes 'flu') and HIV (which causes AIDS).

Bacteria is the plural of bacterium.

I think my brother's a pathogen — he definitely causes disease...

There's only one thing for it here — learn the table. Make sure you know what a pathogen is too.

Q1 Give an example of a virus that affects plants.   [1 mark]

Enzymes

Chemical reactions are what make you work. And enzymes are what make them work.

Enzymes are Catalysts Produced by Living Things

1) Living things have thousands of different chemical reactions going on inside them all the time. These reactions need to be carefully controlled — to get the right amounts of substances in the cells.

2) You can usually make a reaction happen more quickly by raising the temperature. This would speed up the useful reactions but also the unwanted ones too... not good. There's also a limit to how far you can raise the temperature inside a living creature before its cells start getting damaged.

3) So living things produce enzymes that act as biological catalysts.

> A catalyst is a substance which increases the speed of a reaction, without being changed or used up in the reaction.

4) Enzymes reduce the need for high temperatures and we only have enzymes to speed up the useful chemical reactions in the body. These reactions are called metabolic reactions.

5) Enzymes are all proteins and all proteins are made up of chains of amino acids. These chains are folded into unique shapes, which enzymes need to do their jobs (see below).

Enzymes are Very Specific

1) Chemical reactions usually involve things either being split apart or joined together.

2) A substrate is a molecule that is changed in a reaction.

3) Every enzyme molecule has an active site — the part where a substrate joins on to the enzyme.

4) Enzymes are really picky — they usually only speed up one reaction. This is because, for an enzyme to work, a substrate has to be the correct shape to fit into the active site.

5) This is called the 'lock and key' model, because the substrate fits into the enzyme just like a key fits into a lock.

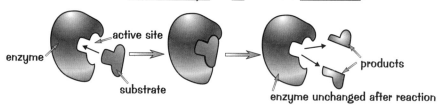

Temperature and pH Affect Enzyme Function

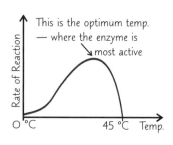

1) Changing the temperature changes the rate of an enzyme-catalysed reaction.

2) Like with any reaction, a higher temperature increases the rate at first. The enzymes and substrate have more energy, so they move about more and are more likely to collide and form enzyme-substrate complexes. But if it gets too hot, some of the bonds holding the enzyme together break. This changes the shape of the enzyme's active site, so the substrate won't fit any more. The enzyme is said to be denatured.

3) All enzymes have an optimum temperature that they work best at.

4) The pH also affects enzymes. If it's too high or too low, the pH interferes with the bonds holding the enzyme together. This changes the shape of the active site and denatures the enzyme.

5) All enzymes have an optimum pH that they work best at. It's often neutral pH 7, but not always.

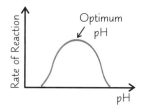

If the lock and key mechanism fails — get in through a window...

Make sure you use the special terms like 'active site' and 'denatured' — the examiners will love it.

Q1   Explain why enzymes have an optimum pH.   [2 marks]

Investigating Enzyme Activity PRACTICAL

You'll soon know how to investigate the effect of a variable on the rate of enzyme activity... I bet you're thrilled.

You Can Investigate How Temperature Affects Enzyme Activity

You Can Measure How Fast a Product Appears...

1) The enzyme catalase catalyses the breakdown of hydrogen peroxide into water and oxygen.

2) You can collect the oxygen and measure how much is produced in a set time.

3) Use a pipette to add a set amount of hydrogen peroxide to a boiling tube. Put the tube in a water bath at 10 °C.

4) Set up the rest of the apparatus as shown. Add a source of catalase (e.g. 1 cm³ of potato) to the hydrogen peroxide and quickly attach the bung.

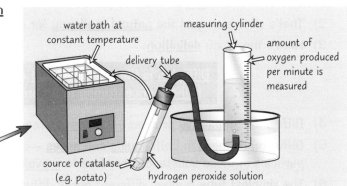

5) Record how much oxygen is produced in the first minute. Repeat three times and calculate the mean.

6) Repeat at 20 °C, 30 °C and 40 °C.

7) Control any variables (e.g. pH, the potato used, the size of potato pieces, etc.) to make it a fair test.

...Or How Fast a Substrate Disappears

1) The enzyme amylase catalyses the breakdown of starch to maltose.

2) It's easy to detect starch using iodine solution — if starch is present, the iodine solution will change from browny-orange to blue-black.

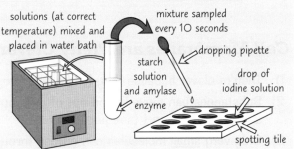

3) Set up the apparatus as in the diagram. Put a drop of iodine solution into each well on the spotting tile. Every ten seconds, drop a sample of the mixture into a well using a pipette. When the iodine solution remains browny-orange (i.e. starch is no longer present) record the total time taken.

4) Repeat with the water bath at different temperatures to see how it affects the time taken for the starch to be broken down. Remember to control all of the variables each time.

You Can Also Investigate How pH Affects Enzyme Activity

1) You can adapt these experiments to investigate the effect of pH on enzyme activity.

2) Follow the same method, but add a buffer solution with a different pH level to a series of different tubes containing the enzyme-substrate mixture.

3) As before, control any variables — use the water bath to keep the temperature of the reaction mixture the same for each pH, and make sure volumes and concentrations are kept the same.

Paper 2

If only enzymes could speed up revision...

The key thing with experiments is to only change the thing you're testing — and absolutely nothing else. Sorted.

Q1 An experiment is carried out to investigate the effect of temperature on the breakdown of hydrogen peroxide by the enzyme catalase. Cubes of potato are used as a source of catalase. Suggest two variables that would need to be controlled in this experiment. [2 marks]

Diffusion

Diffusion is <u>really important</u> in living organisms — it's how a lot of <u>substances</u> get <u>in</u> and <u>out</u> of cells. Basically particles <u>move about randomly</u>, and after a bit they end up <u>evenly spaced</u>.

Diffusion — Don't be Put Off by the Fancy Word

1) <u>Diffusion</u> is simple. It's just the <u>gradual movement</u> of particles from places where there are <u>lots</u> of them to places where there are <u>fewer</u> of them.

2) That's all it is — just the <u>natural tendency</u> for stuff to <u>spread out</u>.

3) Here's the fancy <u>definition</u>:

> Diffusion is the <u>net movement</u> of <u>particles</u> from an area of <u>higher concentration</u> to an area of <u>lower concentration</u>.

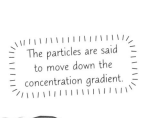

The particles are said to move down the concentration gradient.

4) Diffusion is a <u>passive</u> process — it <u>doesn't</u> require <u>energy</u>.

5) Diffusion happens in both <u>liquids</u> and <u>gases</u> — that's because the particles in these substances are free to <u>move about</u> randomly.

6) The <u>simplest type</u> is when different <u>gases</u> diffuse through each other. This is what's happening when the smell of perfume diffuses through a room:

perfume particles diffused in the air

The <u>bigger</u> the <u>difference</u> in concentration, the <u>faster</u> the diffusion rate.

Cell Membranes are Pretty Clever...

1) They're clever because they <u>hold</u> the cell together <u>but</u> they let stuff <u>in and out</u> as well.

2) Substances can move in and out of cells by <u>diffusion</u>, <u>osmosis</u> (see next page) and <u>active transport</u> (see page 11).

3) Only very <u>small</u> molecules can <u>diffuse</u> through cell membranes though — things like <u>glucose</u>, <u>amino acids</u>, <u>water</u> and <u>oxygen</u>. <u>Big</u> molecules like <u>starch</u> and <u>proteins</u> can't fit through the membrane.

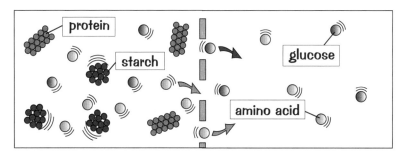

1) Just like with diffusion in air, particles flow through the cell membrane from where there's a <u>higher concentration</u> (more of them) to where there's a <u>lower concentration</u> (not such a lot of them).

2) They're only moving about <u>randomly</u> of course, so they go <u>both</u> ways — but if there are a lot <u>more</u> particles on one side of the membrane, there's a <u>net</u> (overall) movement <u>from</u> that side.

Revision by diffusion — you wish...

Wouldn't that be great — if all the ideas in this book would just gradually drift across into your mind...

Q1 A student adds a drop of ink to a glass of cold water.
What will the student observe happen to the drop of ink? Explain your answer. [2 marks]

Osmosis

If you've got your head round <u>diffusion</u>, osmosis will be a <u>breeze</u>. If not, you need to read the previous page...

Osmosis is a Special Case of Diffusion, That's All

<u>Osmosis</u> is the <u>net movement of water molecules</u> across a <u>partially permeable membrane</u> from a region of <u>higher water concentration</u> to a region of <u>lower water concentration</u>.

You could also describe osmosis as the net movement of water molecules across a partially permeable membrane from a region of lower solute concentration to a region of higher solute concentration.

1) A <u>partially permeable</u> membrane is just one with very small holes in it. So small, in fact, only tiny <u>molecules</u> (like water) can pass through them, and bigger molecules (e.g. <u>sucrose</u>) can't. A <u>cell membrane</u> is a <u>partially permeable</u> membrane.

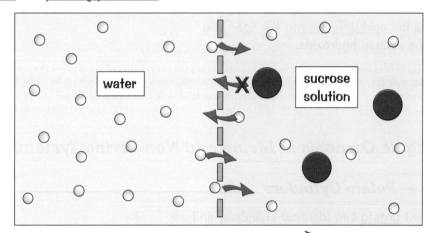

Net movement of water molecules

2) The water molecules actually pass <u>both ways</u> through the membrane during osmosis. This happens because water molecules <u>move about randomly</u> all the time.

3) But because there are <u>more</u> water molecules on one side than on the other, there's a steady <u>net flow</u> of water into the region with <u>fewer</u> water molecules, e.g. into the <u>sucrose</u> solution.

4) This means the <u>sucrose</u> solution gets more <u>dilute</u>. The water acts like it's trying to "<u>even up</u>" the concentration either side of the membrane.

Water Moves Into and Out of Cells by Osmosis

1) <u>Tissue fluid</u> surrounds the cells in the body — it's basically just <u>water</u> with <u>oxygen</u>, <u>glucose</u> and stuff dissolved in it. It's squeezed out of the <u>blood capillaries</u> to supply the cells with everything they need.

2) The tissue fluid will usually have a <u>different concentration</u> to the fluid <u>inside</u> a cell. This means that water will either move <u>into the cell</u> from the tissue fluid, or <u>out of the cell</u>, by <u>osmosis</u>.

3) If a cell is <u>short of water</u>, the solution inside it will become quite <u>concentrated</u>. This usually means the solution <u>outside</u> is more <u>dilute</u>, and so water will move <u>into</u> the cell by osmosis.

4) If a cell has <u>lots of water</u>, the solution inside it will be <u>more dilute</u>, and water will be <u>drawn out</u> of the cell and into the fluid outside by osmosis.

Hope you had your wellies on for this page...

Just remember, osmosis is really just a fancy word for the diffusion of water molecules. It's simple really. And just when you thought that was all for diffusion and osmosis, there are some exciting experiments coming up next...

Q1   Give the definition of osmosis.   [2 marks]

Q2   A cell is short of water. Outline how osmosis will help the cell to gain water.   [2 marks]

Diffusion and Osmosis Experiments

For all you non-believers — here are a few experiments you can do to see diffusion and osmosis in action.

You Can Investigate Diffusion in a Non-Living System

Phenolphthalein is a pH indicator — it's pink in alkaline solutions and colourless in acidic solutions. You can use it to investigate diffusion in agar jelly:

1) First, make up some agar jelly with phenolphthalein and dilute sodium hydroxide. This will make the jelly a lovely shade of pink.

2) Put some dilute hydrochloric acid in a beaker. Cut out a few cubes from the jelly and put them in the beaker of acid.

3) If you leave the cubes for a while they'll eventually turn colourless as the acid diffuses into the agar jelly and neutralises the sodium hydroxide.

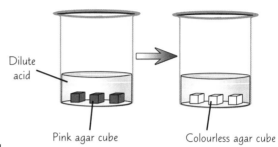

Dilute acid

Pink agar cube

Colourless agar cube

You can investigate the rate of diffusion by using different sized cubes of agar jelly and timing how long it takes for each cube to go colourless. The cube with the largest surface area to volume ratio (see page 11) will lose its colour quickest.

You Can Investigate Osmosis in Living and Non-Living Systems

Living System — Potato Cylinders

Cut up an innocent potato into identical cylinders, and get some beakers with different sugar solutions in them. One should be pure water, another should be a very concentrated sugar solution. Then you can have a few others with concentrations in between. You measure the length of the cylinders, then leave a few cylinders in each beaker for half an hour or so. Then you take them out and measure their lengths again.

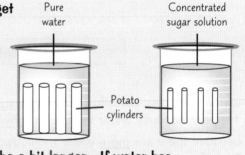

Pure water

Concentrated sugar solution

Potato cylinders

If the cylinders have drawn in water by osmosis, they'll be a bit longer. If water has been drawn out, they'll have shrunk a bit. Then you can plot a few graphs and things.

The only thing that you should change is the concentration of the sugar solution. Everything else (e.g. the volume of solution and the time the experiment runs for) must be kept the same in each case or the experiment won't be a fair test.

Non-living System — Visking Tubing

Fix some Visking tubing over the end of a thistle funnel. Then pour some sugar solution down the glass tube into the thistle funnel.

Put the thistle funnel into a beaker of pure water — measure where the sugar solution comes up to on the glass tube.

Leave the apparatus overnight, then measure where the solution is in the glass tube. Water should be drawn through the Visking tubing by osmosis and this will force the solution up the glass tube.

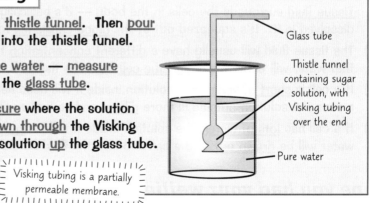

Glass tube

Thistle funnel containing sugar solution, with Visking tubing over the end

Pure water

Visking tubing is a partially permeable membrane.

Jelly, potatoes and Visking tubing — the makings of a good night in...

OK, they weren't the most exciting experiments in the world — but make sure you know how to do them.

Q1   Explain what will happen to the mass of a piece of potato added to a concentrated sugar solution.   [2 marks]

Active Transport

The movement of substances has been too _passive_ for my liking. Put the spandex on — it's time to get _active_.

Active Transport Works Against a Concentration Gradient

Here's what you _need to know_:

> Active Transport is the _movement of particles_ against a concentration gradient (i.e. from an area of _lower concentration_ to an area of _higher concentration_) _using energy_ released during respiration.

Active transport, like diffusion and osmosis, is used to _move substances in and out of cells_. For example, active transport is used in the _digestive system_ when there is a _low concentration_ of nutrients in the _gut_, but a _high concentration_ of nutrients in the _blood_:

1) When there's _a higher concentration_ of nutrients in the gut they _diffuse naturally_ into the blood.

2) _BUT_ — sometimes there's a _lower concentration_ of nutrients in the gut than there is in the blood.

3) This means that the _concentration gradient_ is the wrong way. The nutrients should go _the other way_ if they followed the rules of diffusion.

4) Active transport allows nutrients to be taken into the blood, despite the fact that the _concentration gradient_ is the wrong way. This is essential to stop us starving. But active transport needs _ENERGY_ from _respiration_ to make it work.

> Active transport is also used by plants — it's how they get minerals from the soil (lower mineral concentration) into their root hair cells (higher mineral concentration).

diffusion

active transport

Four Factors Affect The Movement of Substances

The _rates_ of diffusion, osmosis and active transport _vary_ — they're affected by _several factors_:

1) Surface Area to Volume Ratio

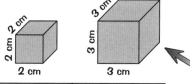

2 cm, 2 cm, 2 cm

3 cm, 3 cm, 3 cm

	2 cm	3 cm
Surface area (cm²)	2 x 2 x 6 = 24	3 x 3 x 6 = 54
Volume (cm³)	2 x 2 x 2 = 8	3 x 3 x 3 = 27
Surface area to volume ratio	24 : 8 = _3 : 1_	54 : 27 = _2 : 1_

This can be a bit _tricky_ to get your head around, but it's easier if you think of cells as _cubes_ for now.

The _rate_ of diffusion, osmosis and active transport is _higher_ in cells (or cubes) with a _larger surface area to volume ratio_.

The _smaller_ cube has a _larger_ surface area to volume ratio — this means _substances_ would _move_ into and out of this cube _faster_.

2) Distance

If substances only have a _short distance_ to move, then they'll move in and out of cells faster. For example, cell membranes are very thin.

3) Temperature

As the particles in a substance get _warmer_ they have _more energy_ — so they _move faster_. This means as _temperature increases_, substances move in and out of cells _faster_.

4) Concentration Gradient

Substances move in and out of a cell _faster_ if there's a _big difference_ in _concentration_ between the inside and outside of the cell (see page 8). If there are _lots more_ particles on one side, there are more there to _move across_. This _only_ increases the rate of _diffusion_ and _osmosis_ though — concentration gradients _don't affect_ the rate of _active transport_.

Bored? Work out the surface area to volume ratio of a loved one...

That's just about it for this section — all that's left for you to do is actively transport yourself to the next page...

Q1 Calculate the surface area to volume ratio of a cube with sides measuring 5 cm. [1 mark]

Revision Questions for Section 1

Well, that's it for Section 1 — time for the first set of questions to see what you've learnt so far.

- Try these questions and tick off each one when you get it right.
- When you've done all the questions for a topic and are completely happy with it, tick off the topic.

Characteristics of Living Organisms and Levels of Organisation (p.1-2) ☐

1) What are the eight basic characteristics that all living organisms share? ☐
2) Name three organelles that are found in both animal and plant cells. Describe their functions. ☐
3) What is a tissue? ☐
4) What is an organ? And an organ system? ☐

Specialised Cells and Stem Cells (p.3) ☐

5) What is cell differentiation? ☐
6) Give two ways that embryonic stem cells could be used to cure diseases. ☐

Plants, Animals and Fungi, and Protoctists, Bacteria and Viruses (p.4-5) ☐

7) What are plant cell walls made of? ☐
8) How do most animals store carbohydrate? ☐
9) Explain what is meant by the term 'saprotrophic nutrition'. ☐
10) Give two examples of protoctists. ☐
11) Give three features of viruses. ☐
12) What are pathogens? Name two pathogens. ☐

Enzymes and Investigating Enzyme Activity (p.6-7) ☐

13) What name is given to biological catalysts? ☐
14) What is a catalyst? ☐
15) What does it mean when an enzyme has been 'denatured'? ☐
16) Briefly describe an experiment to show how
    temperature can affect enzyme activity. ☐
17) In an experiment to investigate how pH can affect enzyme activity,
    outline how you could vary the pH of the reaction mixture. ☐

Diffusion, Osmosis and Active Transport (p.8-11) ☐

18) What is diffusion? ☐
19) What is osmosis? ☐
20) A solution of pure water is separated from a concentrated sucrose solution by a partially permeable
    membrane. In which direction will molecules flow, and what substance will these molecules be? ☐
21) Describe an experiment using a non-living system that shows diffusion taking place.
    Then, as a treat, do the same for osmosis. ☐
22) How is active transport different from diffusion in terms of:
    a) energy requirements,
    b) concentration gradients? ☐
23) Describe how surface area to volume ratio affects the movement of substances in and out of cells. ☐

Biological Molecules and Food Tests

Biological molecules are things like carbohydrates, lipids and proteins. They're generally long, complex molecules made up from smaller basic units. And, unsurprisingly, they're what this page is all about...

You Need to Know the Structure of Carbohydrates, Lipids and Proteins

Carbohydrates are Made Up of Simple Sugars

- Carbohydrate molecules contain the elements carbon, hydrogen and oxygen.
- Starch and glycogen are large, complex carbohydrates, which are made up of many smaller units (e.g. glucose or maltose molecules) joined together in a long chain.

Maltose
and other simple sugars, e.g. glucose

Starch

Proteins are Made Up of Amino Acids

- Proteins are made up of long chains of amino acids.
- They all contain carbon, nitrogen, hydrogen and oxygen atoms.

Amino acids

Proteins

Lipids are Made Up of Fatty Acids and Glycerol

- Lipids (fats and oils) are built from fatty acids and glycerol.
- Lipids contain carbon, hydrogen and oxygen atoms.

Glycerol & fatty acids

Lipid

Before a Food Test, You Need to Make a Food Sample

1) There are some clever ways to identify what type of biological molecule a sample contains.
2) The methods for carrying out these tests are coming up on the next page.
3) However, before you can carry out the tests, you need to prepare a food sample.
4) Here's what you'd do:

1) Get a piece of food and break it up using a pestle and mortar.
2) Transfer the ground up food to a beaker and add some distilled water.
3) Give the mixture a good stir with a glass rod to dissolve some of the food.
4) Filter the solution using a funnel lined with filter paper to get rid of the solid bits of food.

My peanut butter sandwich got top marks in its food test...

It's really important that you remember what carbohydrates, proteins and sugars are made up from — it's going to come up again when you read about digestion so you might as well get it stuck in your brain now. You also need to know how to make a food sample, ready for those food tests coming up on the next page. It's about to get exciting...

Q1   What type of biological molecule is made up of simple sugars?   [1 mark]

Q2   Name the chemical elements that proteins are made up of.   [1 mark]

Q3   Describe how to prepare a food sample for a food test.   [4 marks]

Food Tests

Before you get going with this, make sure you can remember how to prepare a <u>food sample</u>.
If you can't, have a look back to the previous page before you go any further...

Use the Benedict's Test to Test for Glucose

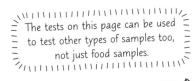

The tests on this page can be used
to test other types of samples too,
not just food samples.

<u>Glucose</u> is found in all sorts of foods such as <u>biscuits</u>, <u>cereal</u> and <u>bread</u>.
You can test for <u>glucose</u> in foods using the <u>Benedict's test</u>:

1) Prepare a <u>food sample</u> and transfer <u>5 cm³</u> to a test tube.

2) Prepare a <u>water bath</u> so that it's set to <u>75 °C</u>.

3) Add some <u>Benedict's solution</u> to the test tube (about <u>10 drops</u>) using a pipette.

4) Place the test tube in the water bath using a test tube holder and leave it in there for <u>5 minutes</u>.
   Make sure the tube is <u>pointing away</u> from you.

5) If the food sample contains <u>glucose</u>, the solution in the test tube will change
   from its normal <u>blue</u> colour. It will become <u>green</u> or <u>yellow</u> in <u>low concentrations</u>
   of glucose, or <u>brick-red</u> in <u>high concentrations</u> of glucose.

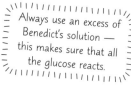

Always use an excess of
Benedict's solution —
this makes sure that all
the glucose reacts.

Use Iodine Solution to Test for Starch

You can also check food samples for the presence of <u>starch</u>. Foods like <u>pasta</u>, <u>rice</u> and <u>potatoes</u> contain
a lot of starch. Here's how to do the test:

1) Make a <u>food sample</u> and transfer <u>5 cm³</u> of your sample to a test tube.

2) Then add a few drops of <u>iodine solution</u> and <u>gently shake</u> the tube to mix the contents. If the sample
   contains starch, the colour of the solution will change from <u>browny-orange</u> to <u>black</u> or <u>blue-black</u>.

Use the Biuret Test to Test for Proteins

You can use the <u>biuret test</u> to see if a type of food contains <u>protein</u>.
<u>Meat</u> and <u>cheese</u> are protein rich and good foods to use in this test. Here's how it's done:

1) Prepare a <u>sample</u> of your food and transfer <u>2 cm³</u> of your sample to a test tube.

2) Add 2 cm³ of <u>biuret solution</u> to the sample and mix the contents of the tube by <u>gently shaking</u> it.

3) If the food sample contains protein, the solution will change from <u>blue</u> to <u>pink</u> or <u>purple</u>.
   If no protein is present, the solution will stay blue.

Use the Sudan III Test to Test for Lipids

<u>Lipids</u> are found in foods such as <u>olive oil</u>, <u>margarine</u> and <u>milk</u>.
You can test for the presence of lipids in a food using <u>Sudan III stain solution</u>.

1) Prepare a <u>sample</u> of the food you're testing (but you don't need to filter it).
   Transfer about <u>5 cm³</u> into a test tube.

2) Use a pipette to add <u>3 drops</u> of <u>Sudan III stain solution</u> to the test tube and <u>gently shake</u> the tube.

3) Sudan III stain solution <u>stains</u> lipids. If the sample contains lipids, the mixture will separate out into
   <u>two layers</u>. The top layer will be <u>bright red</u>. If no lipids are present, no separate red layer will form
   at the top of the liquid.

All this talk of food is making me hungry...

Make sure you do a risk assessment before starting these tests — there are a lot of chemicals to use here.

Q1   Name the chemical that you would use to test a sample for the presence of protein.   [1 mark]

A Balanced Diet

Your body needs the right fuel or it won't work properly — that means cutting down on the lard, I'm afraid...

You Need to Eat Different Foods to Get Different Nutrients

Nutrient		Found in...	Function(s)
Carbohydrates		Pasta, rice, sugar	Provide energy.
Lipids (fats and oils)		Butter, oily fish	Provide energy, act as an energy store and provide insulation.
Proteins		Meat, fish	Needed for growth and repair of tissue, and to provide energy in emergencies.
Vitamins	A	Liver (yum...)	Helps to improve vision and keep your skin and hair healthy.
	C	Fruit, e.g. oranges	Needed to prevent scurvy.
	D	Eggs	Needed for calcium absorption.
Mineral ions	Calcium	Milk, cheese	Needed to make bones and teeth.
	Iron	Red meat	Needed to make haemoglobin for healthy blood.
Water		Food and drink	Just about every bodily function relies on water — we need a constant supply to replace water lost through urinating, breathing and sweating.
Dietary fibre		Wholemeal bread, fruit	Aids the movement of food through the gut.

Vitamin D is also made by your body when your skin is exposed to sunlight.

A Balanced Diet Supplies All Your Essential Nutrients

1) A balanced diet gives you all the essential nutrients you need — in the right proportions.
2) The six essential nutrients are carbohydrates, proteins, lipids, vitamins, minerals and water.
3) You also need fibre (to keep the gut in good working order).

Energy Requirements Vary in Different People

You get energy from the food you eat, but the amount of energy you need isn't a set thing — it's different for everyone. The energy a person needs depends on things like...

Activity level ⟹ Active people need more energy than people who sit about all day. Bit of an obvious one, really...

Age ⟹ Children and teenagers need more energy than older people — they need energy to grow and they're generally more active.

Pregnancy ⟹ Pregnant women need more energy than other women — they've got to provide the energy their babies need to develop.

A plate of protein and carbohydrates, ta — easy on the vitamin A...

Unfortunately, revising food isn't quite as much fun as shovelling it down your gullet. But it's something you've got to do — learn all about the nutrients needed for a balanced diet, then you can treat yourself to a nice biscuit.

Q1   Name one source of vitamin A. [1 mark]

Q2   Describe the function of iron in the diet. [1 mark]

 **Energy From Food**

I bet you've been told many a time not to play with your <u>food</u>. Well for this page I'm going to <u>encourage</u> you to do it, and play with <u>fire</u>, too. Actually it's a pretty <u>fun experiment</u>...

Food Can be Burnt to See How Much Energy it Contains

The posh name for this is <u>calorimetry</u>. You need to know how to do it with a <u>simple experiment</u>:

First You Need a Dry Food, Water and a Flame...

1) You need a <u>food</u> that'll <u>burn easily</u> — something that's <u>dry</u>, e.g. dried beans or pasta, will work best.
2) <u>Weigh</u> a small amount of the food and then <u>skewer</u> it on a <u>mounted needle</u>.
3) Next, add <u>a set volume</u> of <u>water</u> to a boiling tube (held with a clamp) — this will be used to <u>measure</u> the amount of <u>energy</u> that's released when the food is burnt.
4) <u>Measure</u> the <u>temperature</u> of the water, then <u>set fire</u> to the food using a <u>Bunsen burner flame</u>. Make sure the Bunsen isn't near the water or your results might be a bit wonky.
5) Time for the exciting bit — immediately <u>hold</u> the burning food <u>under</u> the boiling tube until it <u>goes out</u>. Then <u>relight</u> the food and <u>hold</u> it under the tube — <u>keep doing this</u> until the food <u>won't</u> catch fire again.
6) The last thing to do is <u>measure</u> the <u>temperature</u> of the water <u>again</u>. Then you're ready for a bit of <u>maths</u>...

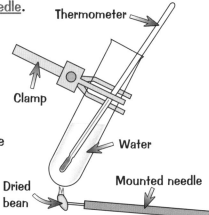

...Then You Can Calculate the Amount of Energy in the Food

① Calculate the Amount of Energy in Joules

$$\text{ENERGY IN FOOD (in J)} = \text{MASS OF WATER (in g)} \times \text{TEMPERATURE CHANGE OF WATER (in °C)} \times 4.2$$

1) <u>1 cm³</u> of water is the same as <u>1 g</u> of water.
2) The <u>4.2</u> in the formula is the <u>amount of energy</u> (in joules) needed to <u>raise</u> the temperature of <u>1 g</u> of water by <u>1 °C</u>. ← This is the specific heat capacity of water, otherwise known as a calorie.

② Calculate the Amount of Energy in Joules per Gram

$$\text{ENERGY PER GRAM OF FOOD (in J/g)} = \frac{\text{ENERGY IN FOOD (in J)}}{\text{MASS OF FOOD (in g)}}$$

You need to do this calculation so you can <u>compare</u> the energy values of different foods <u>fairly</u>.

The Accuracy of the Experiment Can be Increased

1) The experiment <u>isn't perfect</u> — quite a bit of the <u>energy</u> released from burning is <u>lost</u> to the surroundings. It's why the energy value on the <u>packet</u> of the food you used is likely to be <u>much higher</u> than your own.
2) <u>Insulating</u> the boiling tube, e.g. with foil, would minimise heat loss and keep <u>more energy</u> in the water — making your results <u>more accurate</u>.

Try selling the water from this practical as a budget energy drink...

Food scientists use calorimeters to measure food energy. They're well insulated and sealed to minimise heat loss.

Q1   A food sample raises the temperature of 30 g of water by 18 °C.
Calculate the amount of energy in the food sample in Joules.   [1 mark]

Section 2 — Human Nutrition

Enzymes and Digestion

Various enzymes are used in <u>digestion</u> — they're produced by specialised cells and then <u>released</u> into the <u>gut</u>.

Digestive Enzymes Break Down Big Molecules into Smaller Ones

1) <u>Starch</u>, <u>proteins</u> and <u>fats</u> are <u>BIG molecules</u>. They're <u>too big</u> to pass through the <u>walls</u> of the digestive system. They're also <u>insoluble</u>.

2) <u>Sugars</u>, <u>amino acids</u>, <u>glycerol</u> and <u>fatty acids</u> are much smaller molecules. They're <u>soluble</u> and can <u>pass easily</u> through the walls of the digestive system.

3) The <u>digestive enzymes</u> break down the BIG molecules into the smaller ones.

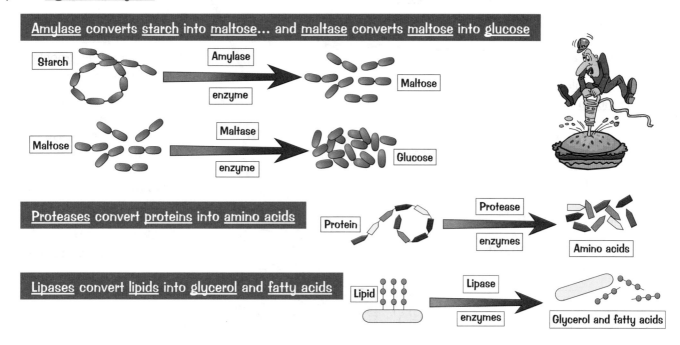

<u>Amylase</u> converts <u>starch</u> into <u>maltose</u>... and <u>maltase</u> converts <u>maltose</u> into <u>glucose</u>

<u>Proteases</u> convert <u>proteins</u> into <u>amino acids</u>

<u>Lipases</u> convert <u>lipids</u> into <u>glycerol</u> and <u>fatty acids</u>

Bile Neutralises the Stomach Acid and Emulsifies Fats

1) Bile is <u>produced</u> in the <u>liver</u>. It's <u>stored</u> in the <u>gall bladder</u> before it's released into the <u>small intestine</u>.

2) The <u>hydrochloric acid</u> in the stomach makes the pH <u>too acidic</u> for enzymes in the small intestine to work properly. Bile is <u>alkaline</u> — it <u>neutralises</u> the acid and makes conditions <u>alkaline</u>. The enzymes in the small intestine <u>work best</u> in these alkaline conditions.

3) Bile also <u>emulsifies</u> fats. In other words it breaks the fat into <u>tiny droplets</u>. This gives a much <u>bigger surface area</u> of fat for the enzyme lipase to work on — which makes its digestion <u>faster</u>.

Food is Moved Through The Gut by Peristalsis

1) There's <u>muscular</u> tissue all the way down the alimentary canal (see next page).

2) Its job is to <u>squeeze</u> balls of food (called boluses) through your gut — <u>otherwise</u> it would get <u>clogged up</u> with bits of old food.

3) This squeezing action, which is <u>waves</u> of <u>circular muscle contractions</u>, is called <u>peristalsis</u>.

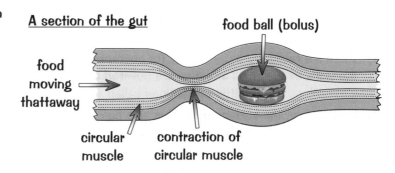

A section of the gut

food ball (bolus)

food moving thattaway

circular muscle

contraction of circular muscle

What do you call an acid that's eaten all the pies...

You need to know which enzymes digest which food molecules. And there's no time like the present...

Q1   Give the name for the muscle action that moves food through the gut.   [1 mark]

The Alimentary Canal

So, now you know what the enzymes do, here's a nice <u>big picture</u> of the <u>whole</u> of your gut.

Your Alimentary Canal Runs Through Your Body

You need to know the names and functions of the alimentary canal's main parts, plus a few of the organs associated with it.

The alimentary canal is another name for the <u>gut</u>.

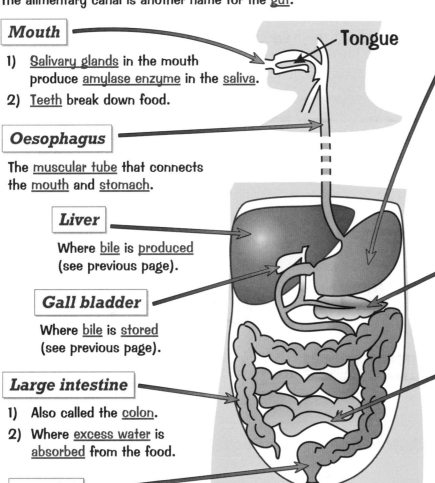

Mouth

1) <u>Salivary glands</u> in the mouth produce <u>amylase enzyme</u> in the <u>saliva</u>.
2) <u>Teeth</u> break down food.

Oesophagus

The <u>muscular tube</u> that connects the <u>mouth</u> and <u>stomach</u>.

Liver

Where <u>bile</u> is <u>produced</u> (see previous page).

Gall bladder

Where <u>bile</u> is <u>stored</u> (see previous page).

Large intestine

1) Also called the <u>colon</u>.
2) Where <u>excess water</u> is <u>absorbed</u> from the food.

Rectum

1) The last part of the <u>large intestine</u>.
2) Where the <u>faeces</u> (made up mainly of indigestible food) are <u>stored</u> before they bid you a fond farewell through the <u>anus</u>.

Stomach

1) It <u>pummels</u> the food with its muscular walls.
2) It produces the <u>protease</u> enzyme, <u>pepsin</u>.
3) It produces <u>hydrochloric acid</u> for two reasons:
   a) To <u>kill bacteria</u>.
   b) To give the <u>optimum pH</u> for the <u>protease</u> enzyme to work (pH 2 — <u>acidic</u>).

Pancreas

Produces <u>protease</u>, <u>amylase</u> and <u>lipase</u> enzymes. It releases these into the <u>small intestine</u>.

Small intestine

1) Produces <u>protease</u>, <u>amylase</u> and <u>lipase</u> enzymes to complete digestion.
2) This is also where the nutrients are <u>absorbed</u> out of the alimentary canal into the body.
3) The first part is the <u>duodenum</u> and the last part is the <u>ileum</u>.

Villi in the Small Intestine Help with Absorption

1) The <u>small intestine</u> is <u>adapted</u> for absorption of food.
2) It's very <u>long</u>, so there's time to break down and absorb <u>all</u> the food before it reaches the end.
3) There's a really <u>big surface area</u> for absorption, because the walls of the small intestine are covered in <u>millions and millions</u> of tiny little projections called <u>villi</u>.
4) Each <u>cell</u> on the surface of a villus also has its own <u>microvilli</u> — little projections that increase the surface area even more.
5) Villi have a <u>single permeable</u> layer of surface cells and a very <u>good blood supply</u> to assist <u>quick absorption</u>.

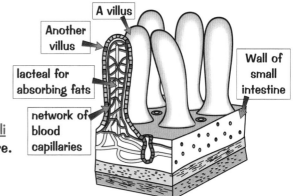

You don't have to bust a gut to revise this page...

This stuff is pretty easy to digest — just make sure you know what all the parts of the alimentary canal do.

Q1   Name two parts of the small intestine.   [2 marks]

Revision Questions for Section 2

That's Section 2 done and dusted. Well, nearly — have a go at these questions before you head off for a cuppa.
- Try these questions and tick off each one when you get it right.
- When you've done all the questions for a topic and are completely happy with it, tick off the topic.

Biological Molecules and Food Tests (p.13-14) ☐

1) Name the three main chemical elements that are found in carbohydrates. ☑
2) What type of biological molecules are made up of:
   a) fatty acids and glycerol?
   b) amino acids? ☑
3) Describe how you could use Benedict's solution to test for glucose. ☑
4) What solution could you use to see if there's starch in a sample? ☑

A Balanced Diet and Energy from Food (p.15-16) ☑

5) What nutrients does the body get energy from? ☑
6) Why does the body need proteins? What foods contain proteins? ☑
7) Eric has just been to see his doctor. He has been told that he needs to increase the amount of vitamin D in his diet. What foods can Eric get this nutrient from? Why does Eric need vitamin D? ☑
8) Explain fully what is meant by the term 'a balanced diet'. ☑
9) Explain the difference in energy requirements between:
   a) children and older people.
   b) a woman who's pregnant and one who isn't. ☑
10) a) Describe a simple experiment to measure the amount of energy in a food.
    b) Give one way you could make the experiment more accurate. ☑

Enzymes, Digestion and the Alimentary Canal (p.17-18) ☑

11) What is the main role of digestive enzymes? ☑
12) Name the enzymes that convert starch into glucose. ☑
13) What do proteases do? ☑
14) When lipids are digested, what molecules are they broken down into? ☑
15) Where in the body is bile:
    a) produced?   b) stored?   c) used? ☑
16) What are the two functions of bile? ☑
17) Describe the function(s) of the:
    a) mouth,
    b) oesophagus,
    c) small intestine. ☑
18) Explain how villi help with absorption in the small intestine. ☑

Photosynthesis

Plants can make their <u>own food</u> — it's <u>ace</u>. Here's how...

Photosynthesis Produces Glucose Using Sunlight

1) <u>Photosynthesis</u> is the process that produces '<u>food</u>' in plants. The 'food' it produces is <u>glucose</u>.

2) Photosynthesis happens in the <u>leaves</u> of all <u>green plants</u> — this is largely what the leaves are for.

3) Photosynthesis happens inside the <u>chloroplasts</u>, which are found in leaf cells and in other <u>green</u> parts of a plant. Chloroplasts contain a pigment called <u>chlorophyll</u>, which absorbs <u>sunlight</u> and uses its energy to convert <u>carbon dioxide</u> and <u>water</u> into <u>glucose</u>. <u>Oxygen</u> is also produced.

You need to learn the <u>word</u> and <u>symbol equations</u> for photosynthesis:

$$\text{carbon dioxide} + \text{water} \xrightarrow[\text{chlorophyll}]{\text{LIGHT}} \text{glucose} + \text{oxygen}$$

$$6CO_2 + 6H_2O \longrightarrow C_6H_{12}O_6 + 6O_2$$

4) Photosynthesis is an important process because it <u>converts light energy to chemical energy</u>, which is <u>stored</u> in the <u>glucose</u>. This chemical energy is <u>released</u> when glucose is broken down during <u>respiration</u> (see page 29).

Leaves are Designed for Making Food by Photosynthesis

The whole structure of leaves is geared towards that. You need to know all the different parts of a <u>typical leaf</u> shown on the diagram:

Funny names here — like mesophyll. Mesophyll just means 'middle of a leaf'. (So why can't they just say that?)

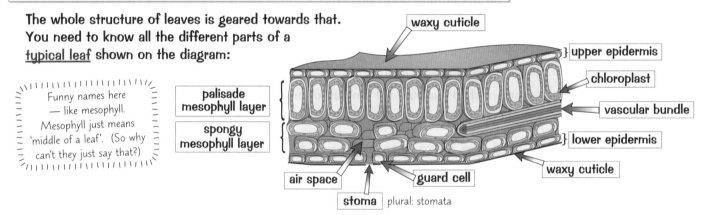

palisade mesophyll layer

spongy mesophyll layer

waxy cuticle

upper epidermis

chloroplast

vascular bundle

lower epidermis

waxy cuticle

air space

guard cell

stoma   plural: stomata

Leaves are Adapted for Efficient Photosynthesis

1) Leaves are <u>broad</u>, so there's a large surface area exposed to <u>light</u>.

2) Most of the chloroplasts are found in the <u>palisade layer</u>. This is so that they're near the top of the leaf where they can get the most <u>light</u>.

3) The <u>upper epidermis</u> is <u>transparent</u> so that light can pass through it to the <u>palisade layer</u>.

4) Leaves have a network of <u>vascular bundles</u> — these are the transport vessels <u>xylem</u> and <u>phloem</u> (see page 25). They <u>deliver water</u> and other <u>nutrients</u> to every part of the leaf and take away the <u>glucose</u> produced by photosynthesis. They also help to <u>support</u> the leaf structure.

5) The <u>waxy cuticle</u> helps to <u>reduce water loss</u> by evaporation.

6) The <u>adaptations</u> of leaves for efficient <u>gas exchange</u> (see page 31) also make <u>photosynthesis</u> more efficient. E.g. the lower surface is full of little holes called <u>stomata</u>, which let CO_2 diffuse directly into the leaf.

I'm working on sunshine — woah oh...

Plants are pretty crucial in ensuring the flow of energy through nature. They're able to use the Sun's energy to make glucose — the energy source which humans and animals need for respiration.

Q1   Name the products of photosynthesis.   [2 marks]

Rate of Photosynthesis

A plant's rate of photosynthesis is affected by the amount of <u>light</u>, the amount of <u>CO_2</u>, and the <u>temperature</u> of its surroundings. Photosynthesis slows down or stops if the conditions aren't right.

The Limiting Factor Depends on the Conditions

1) A limiting factor is something which <u>stops photosynthesis from happening any faster</u>. Light intensity, CO_2 concentration and temperature can all be the limiting factor.

2) The limiting factor depends on the <u>environmental conditions</u>. E.g. in <u>winter</u> low temperatures might be the limiting factor. At <u>night</u>, light is likely to be the limiting factor.

There are Three Important Graphs for Rate of Photosynthesis

1) Not Enough LIGHT Slows Down the Rate of Photosynthesis

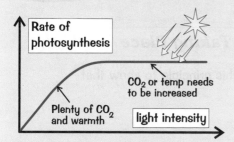

<u>Chlorophyll</u> uses <u>light energy</u> to perform photosynthesis. It can only do it as quickly as the light energy is arriving.

1) If the <u>light intensity</u> is increased, the rate of photosynthesis will <u>increase steadily</u>, but only up to a <u>certain point</u>.

2) Beyond that, it won't make any <u>difference</u> because then it'll be either the <u>temperature</u> or the <u>CO_2</u> level which is now the limiting factor.

2) Too Little CARBON DIOXIDE Also Slows It Down

<u>CO_2</u> is one of the <u>raw materials</u> needed for photosynthesis — only <u>0.04%</u> of the air is CO_2, so it's <u>pretty scarce</u> as far as plants are concerned.

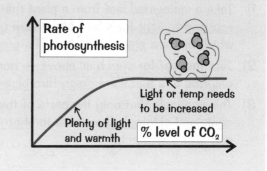

1) As with light intensity, increasing the concentration of CO_2 will only <u>increase</u> the rate of photosynthesis up to a point. After this the graph <u>flattens out</u>, showing that CO_2 is no longer the limiting factor.

2) As long as <u>light</u> and <u>CO_2</u> are in plentiful supply then the factor limiting photosynthesis must be <u>temperature</u>.

3) The TEMPERATURE Has to be Just Right

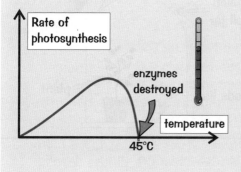

Temperature affects the rate of photosynthesis — because it affects the <u>enzymes</u> involved.

1) As the <u>temperature increases</u>, so does the <u>rate</u> of photosynthesis — up to a point.

2) If the temperature is <u>too high</u> (over about 45 °C), the plant's <u>enzymes</u> will be <u>denatured</u> (destroyed), so the rate of photosynthesis rapidly decreases.

3) <u>Usually</u> though, if the temperature is the <u>limiting factor</u> it's because it's too low, and things need <u>warming up a bit</u>.

Don't blame it on the sunshine, don't blame it on the CO₂...

...don't blame it on the temperature, blame it on the plant. And now you'll never forget these three limiting factors in photosynthesis. No... well, make sure you read this page over and over again 'til you're sure you won't.

Q1   Explain the effect of increasing temperature on the rate of photosynthesis.   [3 marks]

PRACTICAL | Photosynthesis Experiments

The <u>two products</u> from photosynthesis are <u>glucose</u> and <u>oxygen</u> (see page 20). Glucose is stored by plants as <u>starch</u>. You can test for starch (see below) and oxygen (see next page) to <u>investigate photosynthesis</u>.

You Need to Know How to Test a Leaf for Starch

1) Start by dunking the leaf in boiling water (hold it with tweezers or forceps). This <u>stops</u> any <u>chemical reactions</u> happening inside the leaf.

2) Now put the leaf in a boiling tube with some <u>ethanol</u> and heat it in an electric water bath until it boils — this gets rid of any <u>chlorophyll</u> and makes the leaf a <u>white-ish</u> colour.

3) Finally, <u>rinse</u> the leaf in <u>cold water</u> and add a few drops of <u>iodine solution</u> — if <u>starch</u> is <u>present</u> the leaf will turn <u>blue-black</u>.

> Ethanol is highly flammable — keep it away from naked flames, e.g. Bunsen burners.

The Starch Test Shows Whether Photosynthesis is Taking Place

If a plant can't <u>photosynthesise</u>, it can't make <u>starch</u>. You can use this principle to show that <u>chlorophyll</u> and <u>CO_2</u> are <u>needed for photosynthesis</u>. Here's how...

Chlorophyll

You can show that <u>chlorophyll</u> is needed for photosynthesis using <u>variegated</u> (green and white) <u>leaves</u>. Only the <u>green parts</u> of the leaf contain <u>chlorophyll</u>.

1) Take a variegated leaf from a plant that's been <u>exposed to light</u> for a bit. Make sure you <u>record</u> which bits are <u>green</u> and which bits <u>aren't</u>.

2) Test the leaf for starch as above — you'll see that only the bits that were <u>green</u> turn <u>blue-black</u>.

3) This suggests that only the parts of the leaf that <u>contained chlorophyll</u> are able to <u>photosynthesise</u> and <u>produce starch</u>.

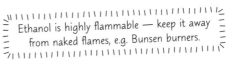

chlorophyll

no chlorophyll

starch absent

starch present

Variegated leaf before testing

Variegated leaf after testing

> The white parts of the leaf go yellow/orange because the brown iodine solution stains them.

> For both of these tests, it's important that any variables that could affect the results, e.g. the temperature, are controlled.

CO_2

1) You can show that <u>CO_2</u> is needed for photosynthesis with the apparatus shown on the right.

2) The soda lime will <u>absorb CO_2</u> out of the air in the jar.

3) If you leave the plant in the jar for a while and then <u>test</u> a leaf for starch, it <u>won't</u> turn blue-black.

4) This shows that <u>no starch</u> has been made in the leaf, which means that <u>CO_2 is needed</u> for photosynthesis.

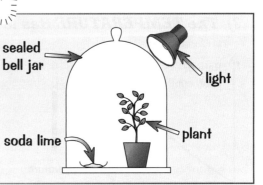

sealed bell jar

light

plant

soda lime

Some like it hot — apparently plant leaves don't...

Mass boiling of plant leaves is required here. It kind of gives you a snapshot of what's going on inside the leaf as it stops all the chemical reactions that are taking place. Then you're free to do some lovely starch testing. Admit it, you're excited... You're not? Well don't tell the plant that you nicked all the leaves for these tests from then...

Q1   Name the chemical used to test for starch.   [1 mark]

More Photosynthesis Experiments PRACTICAL

More starch testing on this page I'm afraid. But there's also a bit about how oxygen production can show the rate of photosynthesis. Don't say I don't mix things up a bit for you...

The Starch Test Shows Whether Photosynthesis is Taking Place

Remember, if a plant can't photosynthesise, it can't make starch. You can use this principle to show that light is needed for photosynthesis. Here's how:

1) To show that light is needed for photosynthesis you need a plant that's been grown without any light, e.g. in a cupboard for 48 hours. This will mean that it has used up its starch stores.

2) Cut a leaf from the plant and test it for starch using iodine solution (see previous page) — the leaf won't turn blue-black.

3) This shows that light is needed for photosynthesis, as no starch has been made.

Even though the plant is kept in the dark, you need to make sure it's warm enough to photosynthesise and that there's plenty of CO_2 — or it won't be a fair test.

Oxygen Production Shows the Rate of Photosynthesis

Canadian pondweed can be used to measure the effect of light intensity on the rate of photosynthesis. The rate at which the pondweed produces oxygen corresponds to the rate at which it's photosynthesising — the faster the rate of oxygen production, the faster the rate of photosynthesis.

Here's how the experiment works:

1) The apparatus is set up according to the diagram. The gas syringe should be empty to start with. Sodium hydrogencarbonate may be added to the water to make sure the plant has enough carbon dioxide (it releases CO_2 in solution).

2) A source of white light is placed at a specific distance from the pondweed.

3) The pondweed is left to photosynthesise for a set amount of time. As it photosynthesises, the oxygen released will collect in the capillary tube.

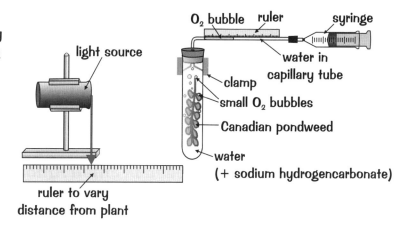

4) At the end of the experiment, the syringe is used to draw the gas bubble in the tube up alongside a ruler and the length of the gas bubble is measured. This is proportional to the volume of O_2 produced.

5) For this experiment, any variables that could affect the results should be controlled, e.g. the temperature and time the pondweed is left to photosynthesise.

6) The experiment is then repeated with the light source placed at different distances from the pondweed.

The apparatus above can be altered to measure the effect of temperature and CO_2 on photosynthesis, e.g. the test tube of pondweed is put into a beaker of water at a set temperature and CO_2 is bubbled into the test tube (then the experiment's repeated with different temperatures of water or concentrations of CO_2).

Canadian pondweed, eh — I bet the British stuff feels a bit left out...

Poor old plant in the dark... I think the pondweed gets a much better deal, floating around in a nice, clean test tube. Anyway, the main points here are that plants in the dark won't produce any starch and that you can use pondweed to investigate oxygen production from a photosynthesising plant. Cool.

Q1   Explain how the starch test can be used to show that plants need light to photosynthesise.   [4 marks]

Minerals for Healthy Growth

Plants are important in food chains and nutrient cycles because they can take minerals from the soil and energy from the Sun and turn it into food. And then, after all that hard work, we eat them — it seems a little unfair, but that's the way of the world. Anyway, learn this page — it's important for healthy brain growth.

Plants Need Three Main Mineral Ions For Growth

1) Plants need certain elements so they can produce important compounds.
2) They get these elements from mineral ions in the soil.
3) If there aren't enough of these mineral ions in the soil, plants suffer deficiency symptoms.

1) Nitrates

Contain nitrogen for making amino acids and proteins. These are needed for cell growth. If a plant can't get enough nitrates it will be stunted and older leaves will turn yellow.

2) Phosphates

Contain phosphorus for making DNA and cell membranes and they're needed for respiration and growth. Plants without enough phosphate have poor root growth and their older leaves are purple.

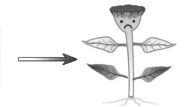

3) Potassium

To help the enzymes needed for photosynthesis and respiration. If there's not enough potassium in the soil, plants have poor flower and fruit growth and discoloured leaves.

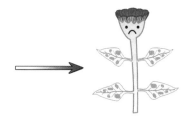

Magnesium is Also Needed in Small Amounts

1) The three main mineral ions are needed in fairly large amounts, but there are other elements which are needed in much smaller amounts.

2) Magnesium is one of the most significant as it's required for making chlorophyll (needed for photosynthesis).

3) Plants without enough magnesium have yellow leaves.

Symptoms of revision deficiency — nagging parents, poor grades...

When a farmer or a gardener buys fertiliser, that's pretty much what he or she is buying — nitrates, phosphates and potassium. A fertiliser's NPK label tells you the relative proportions of nitrogen (N), phosphorus (P) and potassium (K) it contains, so you can choose the right one for your plants and soil. Don't forget about magnesium, though — it's dead important that plants get a little bit of this, so that they can make chlorophyll.

Q1   Outline why nitrate ions are needed by plants.   [2 marks]

Q2   Explain why plants lacking in magnesium are less able to photosynthesise.   [1 mark]

Transport in Plants

You might be surprised to learn that there <u>aren't</u> tiny trucks that transport substances around plants. Then again, you might not be — either way, you need to <u>learn</u> the stuff on this page...

Multicellular Organisms Need Transport Systems

1) The <u>cells</u> in all living organisms need a variety of <u>substances</u> to <u>live</u>, e.g. plant cells need things like <u>water</u>, <u>minerals</u> and <u>sugars</u>. They also need to <u>get rid of waste substances</u>.

2) In <u>unicellular</u> organisms, these substances can <u>diffuse directly</u> into and out of the cell across the cell membrane. The diffusion rate is <u>quick</u> because of the <u>short distances</u> substances have to travel.

3) But in <u>multicellular</u> organisms (like animals and plants) <u>direct diffusion</u> from the outer surface would be <u>too slow</u> — that's because substances would have to travel <u>large distances</u> to reach every single cell.

4) So multicellular organisms <u>need transport systems</u> to move substances to and from individual cells <u>quickly</u>.

However, carbon dioxide diffuses into plants at the leaves (where it's needed).

Plants Have Two Main Transport Systems

Plants have <u>two</u> systems transporting stuff around.
<u>Both</u> go to <u>every part</u> of the plant, but they're totally <u>separate</u>.

Xylem tubes transport water and minerals:

The xylem carry <u>water</u> and <u>mineral salts</u> from the <u>roots</u> up the shoot to the leaves in the <u>transpiration stream</u> (see next page).

Water and minerals

Phloem tubes transport food:

1) The phloem transport sugars, like <u>sucrose</u>, and <u>amino acids</u> from where they're made in the leaves to other parts of the plant.

2) This movement of food substances around the plant is known as <u>translocation</u>.

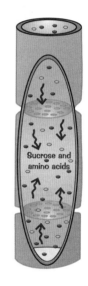

Sucrose and amino acids

Root Hairs Take In Water

1) The cells on plant roots grow into long '<u>hairs</u>' which stick out into the soil.

2) Each branch of a root will be covered in <u>millions</u> of these microscopic hairs.

3) This gives the plant a <u>big surface area</u> for <u>absorbing water</u> from the soil.

Root hair cells also take in minerals — this is done by active transport (see page 11).

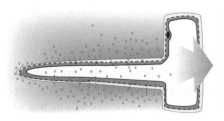

Water is taken in by osmosis (see page 9).
There's usually a <u>higher concentration</u> of water in the <u>soil</u> than there is inside the plant, so the water is <u>drawn into</u> the root hair cell by <u>osmosis</u>.

Paper 2

Don't let revision stress you out — just go with the phloem...

You probably did that really dull experiment at school where you stick a piece of celery in a beaker of water with red food colouring in it. Then you stare at it for half an hour, and once the time is up, hey presto, the red has reached the top of the celery. That's because it travelled there in the xylem. Isn't science amazing...

Q1   Name the vessels that supply sucrose and amino acids to the parts of plants that need them.   [1 mark]

Transpiration

If you don't water a house plant for a few days it starts to go <u>all droopy</u>. Then it <u>dies</u>, and the people from the Society for the Protection of Plants come round and have you <u>arrested</u>. Plants need water.

Transpiration is the Loss of Water from the Plant

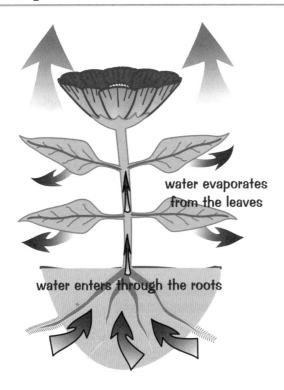

water evaporates from the leaves

water enters through the roots

1) Transpiration is caused by the <u>evaporation</u> and <u>diffusion</u> (see page 8) of water from a plant's surface. Most transpiration happens at the <u>leaves</u>.

2) This evaporation creates a slight <u>shortage</u> of water in the leaf, and so more water is drawn up from the rest of the plant through the <u>xylem vessels</u> (see previous page) to replace it.

3) This in turn means more water is drawn up from the <u>roots</u>, and so there's a constant <u>transpiration stream</u> of water through the plant.

Transpiration is just a <u>side-effect</u> of the way leaves are adapted for <u>photosynthesis</u>. They have to have <u>stomata</u> in them so that gases can be exchanged easily (see page 31). Because there's more water <u>inside</u> the plant than in the <u>air outside</u>, the water escapes from the leaves through the stomata by diffusion.

Transpiration Rate is Affected by Four Main Things

1) <u>LIGHT INTENSITY</u> — the <u>brighter</u> the light, the <u>greater</u> the transpiration rate.

   <u>Stomata</u> begin to <u>close</u> as it gets darker. Photosynthesis can't happen in the dark, so they don't need to be open to let CO_2 in. When the stomata are closed, very little water can escape.

2) <u>TEMPERATURE</u> — the <u>warmer</u> it is, the <u>faster</u> transpiration happens.

   When it's warm the water particles have <u>more energy</u> to evaporate and diffuse out of the stomata.

3) <u>WIND SPEED</u> — the <u>higher</u> the wind speed around a leaf, the <u>greater</u> the transpiration rate.

   If wind speed around a leaf is <u>low</u>, the water vapour just <u>surrounds the leaf</u> and doesn't move away. This means there's a <u>high concentration</u> of water particles outside the leaf as well as inside it, so <u>diffusion</u> doesn't happen as quickly. If it's windy, the water vapour is <u>swept away</u>, maintaining a <u>low concentration</u> of water in the air outside the leaf. Diffusion then happens quickly, from an area of high concentration to an area of low concentration.

4) <u>HUMIDITY</u> — the <u>drier</u> the air around a leaf, the <u>faster</u> transpiration happens.

   This is like what happens with air movement. If the air is <u>humid</u> there's a lot of water in it already, so there's not much of a <u>difference</u> between the inside and the outside of the leaf. Diffusion happens <u>fastest</u> if there's a <u>really high concentration</u> in one place, and a <u>really low concentration</u> in the other.

Transpiration — the plant version of perspiration...

One good way to remember those four factors that affect the rate of transpiration is to think about drying washing. Then you'll realise there are far more boring things you could be doing than revision, and you'll try harder. No, only joking — it's the same stuff: sunny, warm, windy and dry.

Q1   Explain how low light intensity affects the rate of transpiration.   [3 marks]

Paper 2

Measuring Transpiration

PRACTICAL

It's time for another experiment — you get to use a piece of equipment you've probably never heard of...

A Potometer can be Used to Estimate Transpiration Rate

A potometer is a special piece of apparatus used to estimate transpiration rates. It actually measures water uptake by a plant, but it's assumed that water uptake by the plant is directly related to water loss by the leaves (transpiration). Here's how to use a potometer:

1) Cut a shoot underwater to prevent air from entering the xylem. Cut it at a slant to increase the surface area available for water uptake.

2) Assemble the potometer in water and insert the shoot under water, so no air can enter.

3) Remove the apparatus from the water but keep the end of the capillary tube submerged in a beaker of water.

4) Check that the apparatus is watertight and airtight.

5) Dry the leaves, allow time for the shoot to acclimatise and then shut the tap.

6) Remove the end of the capillary tube from the beaker of water until one air bubble has formed, then put the end of the tube back into the water.

7) Record the starting position of the air bubble.

8) Start a stopwatch and record the distance moved by the bubble per unit time, e.g. per hour.

9) Keep the conditions constant throughout the experiment, e.g. the temperature and air humidity.

Setting up a potometer is tough — if there are air bubbles in the apparatus or the plant's xylem it will affect your results.

reservoir of water

Tap is shut off during experiment.

As the plant takes up water, the air bubble moves along the scale.

Water moves this way.

Bubble moves this way.

capillary tube with a scale

Beaker of water.

You Can See How Environmental Conditions Affect Transpiration Rates

You can use a potometer to estimate how different factors affect the transpiration rate. The set up above will be your control — you can vary an environmental condition (see below), run the experiment again and compare the results to the control to see how the change affected the transpiration rate.

Light intensity

You could use a lamp to increase the intensity of light that hits the plant — this should increase the transpiration rate. To decrease the light intensity, put the potometer in a cupboard (this should decrease the transpiration rate).

The size of plant you use should be the same as the size of plant used in your control, to make it a fair test.

Temperature

You could increase or decrease the temperature by putting the potometer in a room that's warmer or colder than where you did the control experiment. An increase in temperature should increase the transpiration rate and a decrease in temperature should lower it.

Humidity

You could increase the humidity of the air around the plant by spraying a little water into a clear plastic bag before sealing it around the plant. This should decrease the rate of transpiration.

Wind speed

You could use a fan to increase the wind speed around the plant — this should increase the transpiration rate.

Potometer — doesn't measure if something is a pot or not...

The tricky bit of using a potometer is setting it up — keeping air out and water in is harder than it sounds.

Q1 Give two variables you should keep constant if investigating the effect of temperature on transpiration rate.

[2 marks]

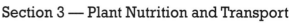

Paper 2

Revision Questions for Section 3

That's <u>Section 3</u> sorted. Before you stride on to the next section though, have a go at these questions.
- Try these questions and <u>tick off each one</u> when you <u>get it right</u>.
- When you've done <u>all the questions</u> for a topic and are <u>completely happy</u> with it, tick off the topic.

<u>Photosynthesis and the Rate of Photosynthesis (p.20-21)</u>

1) Write down the word and balanced symbol equations for photosynthesis.
2) How does being broad help a leaf to photosynthesise?
3) Describe one other way that leaves are adapted for efficient photosynthesis.
4) What is meant by a 'limiting factor' of photosynthesis?
5) What effect would a low carbon dioxide concentration have on the rate of photosynthesis?

<u>Photosynthesis Experiments (p.22-23)</u>

6) Briefly describe an experiment to show that chlorophyll is required for photosynthesis.
7) Describe an experiment that you could carry out to see how light intensity affects the rate of photosynthesis.

<u>Minerals for Healthy Growth (p.24)</u>

8) Name the three main mineral ions plants need for healthy growth.
9) Which mineral ion is needed by plants to make chlorophyll?
10) How can you tell by looking at a plant that it isn't getting enough magnesium?

<u>Transport in Plants and Transpiration (p.25-27)</u>

11) Explain why plants and animals need transport systems to move substances around their bodies but unicellular organisms don't.
12) What is the function of xylem vessels in plants?
13) What is the function of phloem vessels in plants?
14) How does water get into a plant through its root hair cells?
15) What is transpiration?
16) How is the transpiration rate affected by:
    a) increased temperature,
    b) increased humidity?
17) Describe an experiment that you could do to measure how temperature affects the transpiration rate of a plant.

Respiration

You need <u>energy</u> to keep your body going. Energy comes from <u>food</u>, and it's <u>transferred</u> by <u>respiration</u>.

Respiration is NOT "Breathing In and Out"

1) <u>Respiration</u> is the process of transferring energy from <u>glucose</u>. It goes on in <u>every cell</u> in your body.
2) Some of the energy is transferred by <u>heat</u>.
3) The energy transferred by respiration <u>can't</u> be used directly by cells — so it's used to make a substance called <u>ATP</u>. ATP <u>stores the energy</u> needed for many <u>cell processes</u>.
4) When a cell <u>needs energy</u>, ATP molecules are <u>broken down</u> and energy is <u>released</u>.
5) There are <u>two types</u> of respiration, <u>aerobic</u> and <u>anaerobic</u>.

> Respiration is the process of <u>transferring energy</u> from <u>glucose</u>, which happens constantly <u>in every living cell</u>.

Aerobic Respiration Needs Plenty of Oxygen

1) <u>Aerobic respiration</u> is what happens when there's <u>plenty of oxygen</u> available.
2) <u>Aerobic</u> just means "<u>with oxygen</u>" and it's the most efficient way to transfer <u>energy</u> from <u>glucose</u>. It produces <u>lots</u> of <u>ATP</u> — <u>32 molecules</u> per molecule of glucose.
3) This is the type of respiration that you're using <u>most of the time</u>.
   You need to learn the <u>word equation</u> and the <u>balanced chemical equation</u>:

> glucose + oxygen $\longrightarrow$ carbon dioxide + water (+ energy)
> $C_6H_{12}O_6 + 6O_2 \longrightarrow 6CO_2 + 6H_2O$

This is the reverse of the photosynthesis equation (see page 20).

Anaerobic Respiration Doesn't Use Oxygen At All

1) When you do really <u>vigorous exercise</u> your body can't supply enough <u>oxygen</u> to your muscles for aerobic respiration — even though your <u>heart rate</u> and <u>breathing rate</u> increase as much as they can. Your muscles have to start <u>respiring anaerobically</u> as well.
2) <u>Anaerobic</u> just means "<u>without</u> oxygen". It's <u>NOT</u> the best way to convert glucose into energy — it releases much <u>less energy</u> per glucose molecule than aerobic respiration (just <u>2 molecules</u> of ATP are produced).
3) In anaerobic respiration, the glucose is only <u>partially</u> broken down, and <u>lactic acid</u> is also produced.
4) The <u>lactic acid</u> builds up in the muscles — it gets <u>painful</u> and leads to <u>cramp</u>.
   You need to learn the <u>word equation</u> for anaerobic respiration in <u>animals</u>:

Lactic acid can be removed from the muscles by the blood flowing through them.

> glucose $\longrightarrow$ lactic acid (+ energy)

Anaerobic Respiration in Plants is Slightly Different

1) <u>Plants</u> can respire <u>without oxygen</u> too, but they produce <u>ethanol</u> (alcohol) and CO_2 <u>instead</u> of lactic acid.
2) You need to learn the <u>word equation</u> for anaerobic respiration in <u>plants</u>:

Fungi, like yeast, also respire anaerobically like this — and people use yeast to make bread rise (see page 83).

> glucose $\longrightarrow$ ethanol + carbon dioxide (+ energy)

I reckon aerobics classes should be called anaerobics instead...

You need to be able to compare anaerobic and aerobic respiration for your exam. Remember, anaerobic respiration has different products to aerobic respiration and transfers much less energy, as well as taking place without oxygen.

Q1 After one minute of intense sprinting, a runner got cramp in his leg. Explain what caused this. [3 marks]

 # Investigating Respiration

Still not convinced that <u>respiration</u> produces <u>carbon dioxide</u> and transfers some energy by <u>heat</u>?
Well here's the proof. Don't eat all the <u>beans</u>...

Carbon Dioxide Production can be Detected using an Indicator

1) You can use <u>hydrogen-carbonate indicator</u> to show that living organisms produce CO_2 as they respire.
2) Normally this solution is <u>orange</u>, but it <u>changes colour</u> to a <u>lovely yellow</u> in the presence of <u>carbon dioxide</u>.
3) Here's how you can set up an experiment to demonstrate <u>carbon dioxide production</u> by some <u>beans</u>:

First, <u>soak</u> some <u>dried beans</u> in <u>water</u> for a day or two.
They will start to <u>germinate</u> (you should see little sprouts coming out of them). Germinating beans will <u>respire</u>.

<u>Boil</u> a <u>similar-sized</u>, second bunch of dried beans.
This will <u>kill the beans</u> and make sure they <u>can't respire</u>.
The dead beans will act as your <u>control</u>.

Now, set up the experiment as shown on the right:
- Put the same amount of <u>hydrogen-carbonate indicator</u> into two <u>test tubes</u>.
- Place a <u>platform</u> made of <u>gauze</u> into each test tube and place the beans on this.
- <u>Seal</u> the test tubes with a <u>rubber bung</u>.
- Leave the apparatus for a <u>set period</u> of <u>time</u> (e.g. an hour).
- During that time the CO_2 produced by the germinating beans should have had an effect on the <u>hydrogen-carbonate indicator</u> — it will have turned <u>yellow</u>.

germinating beans on gauze
hydrogen-carbonate indicator
One hour later
Test tube

boiled beans on gauze
One hour later
Control tube

4) You could also carry out this experiment with <u>small organisms</u> like woodlice or maggots (the control for these would be glass beads though).

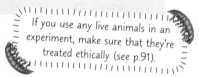 *If you use any live animals in an experiment, make sure that they're treated ethically (see p.91).*

The Temperature Change Produced by Respiration can be Measured

You saw on the previous page that <u>respiration</u> transfers some energy by <u>heat</u> (that's why <u>running</u> makes you get <u>hot</u>) — well here's an experiment to show that. You'll be glad to know it uses more <u>dried beans</u>.

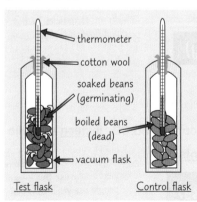
thermometer
cotton wool
soaked beans (germinating)
boiled beans (dead)
vacuum flask
Test flask   Control flask

- Firstly, prepare <u>two sets of beans</u> as described in the experiment above.
- Add each set of beans to a <u>vacuum flask</u>, making sure there's some <u>air</u> left in the flasks (so the beans can <u>respire aerobically</u>).
- Place a <u>thermometer</u> into each flask and seal the top with <u>cotton wool</u>.
- Record the <u>temperature</u> of each flask daily for a week.
- <u>Repeats</u> should be carried out, using the same mass of beans each time.
- The beans are well-insulated in the flasks, so when the germinating beans <u>respire</u>, the <u>test flask's temperature</u> will <u>increase</u> compared to the control flask.

My results are odd — maybe using baked beans wasn't a good idea...

Controls are mega important in experiments — they check that the thing you're observing (e.g. respiring beans) is what's affecting the results and nothing else. So you should make sure everything else is kept exactly the same.

Q1   Describe an investigation using dried beans to show that respiration produces carbon dioxide.   [6 marks]

Gas Exchange — Flowering Plants

Now's a good time to flick back to page 8 and make sure that you thoroughly know about diffusion.

Plants Exchange Gases By Diffusion

1) When plants photosynthesise they use up CO_2 from the atmosphere and produce O_2 as a waste product. When plants respire they use up O_2 and produce CO_2 as a waste product. These waste products are lost through little holes in the undersides of leaves called stomata.

2) So there are lots of gases moving to and fro in plants, and this movement happens by diffusion. E.g.

- When a plant is photosynthesising it uses up lots of CO_2, so there's hardly any inside the leaf. Luckily this makes more CO_2 move into the leaf by diffusion (from an area of higher concentration to an area of lower concentration).

- At the same time lots of O_2 is being made as a waste product of photosynthesis. Some is used in respiration, and the rest diffuses out through the stomata (moving from an area of higher concentration to an area of lower concentration).

The Net Exchange of Gases Depends on Light Intensity

1) Photosynthesis only happens during the day (i.e. when there's light available). But plants must respire all the time, day and night, to get the energy they need to live.

2) During the day (when light intensity is high) plants make more oxygen by photosynthesis than they use in respiration. So in daylight, they release oxygen. They also use up more carbon dioxide than they produce, so they take in carbon dioxide.

3) At night though (or when light intensity is low) plants only respire — there's not enough light for photosynthesis. This means they take in oxygen and release carbon dioxide — just like us.

Leaves are Adapted for Efficient Gas Exchange

1) Leaves are broad, so there's a large surface area for diffusion.

2) They're also thin, so gases only have to travel a short distance to reach the cells where they're needed.

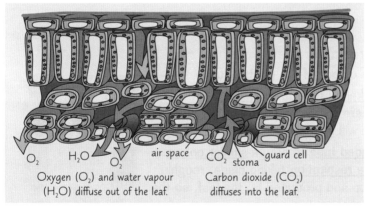

Oxygen (O_2) and water vapour (H_2O) diffuse out of the leaf.

Carbon dioxide (CO_2) diffuses into the leaf.

3) There are air spaces inside the leaf. This lets gases like carbon dioxide and oxygen move easily between cells. It also increases the surface area for gas exchange.

4) The lower surface is full of little holes called stomata. They're there to let gases like CO_2 and O_2 diffuse in and out. They also allow water to escape — which is known as transpiration (see page 26).

5) Stomata begin to close as it gets dark. Photosynthesis can't happen in the dark, so they don't need to be open to let CO_2 in. When the stomata are closed, water can't escape. This stops the plant drying out.

6) Stomata also close when supplies of water from the roots start to dry up. This stops the plant from photosynthesising (bad), but if they didn't close, the plant might dry out and die (worse).

7) The opening and closing of stomata is controlled by the cells that surround them (called guard cells). Guard cells do this by changing their shape and volume. Guard cells increase in volume to open stomata and decrease in volume to close stomata.

Paper 2

I say stomaaarta, you say stomaaayta...

Remember, photosynthesis only happens when light intensity is high, but respiration happens all the time.

Q1   How are the waste gases produced in respiration and photosynthesis lost from the leaf?   [1 mark]

Paper 2

PRACTICAL | Gas Exchange — Flowering Plants

Like the sprinter who forgot to tie his shoes, the experiments are coming thick and fast now. Here's one to measure gas exchange in plants — if you skipped the previous page, I'd go back and read it if I were you.

Hydrogen-carbonate Indicator Shows Changes in CO_2 Concentration...

1) You might remember from p.30 that a solution of hydrogen-carbonate indicator in air with a normal CO_2 concentration is orange.

2) Well if the CO_2 concentration of the air increases, more CO_2 will dissolve in it, and it becomes more yellow.

3) And if the CO_2 concentration of the air decreases, CO_2 will come out of the solution, and it becomes purple.

...So You Can Use it to Show Differences in Net Gas Exchange in Plants

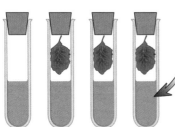

Here's an experiment to show how light affects gas exchange:

1) Add the same volume of hydrogen-carbonate indicator to four boiling tubes.

2) Put similar-sized, healthy-looking leaves into three of the tubes and seal with a rubber bung. Trap the leaf stem with the bung to stop it falling down into the solution if you need to. Keep the fourth tube empty as a control.

3) Completely wrap one tube in aluminium foil, and a second tube in gauze.

4) Place all the tubes in bright light. This will let plenty of light on to the uncovered leaf, and a little light onto the leaf covered in gauze. The leaf covered in foil will get no light — assuming you've wrapped it up properly.

5) Leave the tubes for an hour, then check the colour of the indicator.

control   foil   gauze   uncovered

And The Results are in...

1) There shouldn't be any change in the colour of the control tube.

2) You'd expect the indicator in the darkened tube to go yellow. Respiration will still take place but there will be no photosynthesis, so the CO_2 concentration in the tube will increase.

3) You'd expect the indicator in the shaded tube to stay a similar colour. With a little photosynthesis and some respiration taking place, roughly equal amounts of CO_2 will be taken up and produced by the leaf, so the CO_2 concentration in the tube won't change very much.

4) You'd expect the indicator in the well-lit tube to go purple. There will be some respiration, but lots of photosynthesis, leading to net uptake of CO_2 by the leaf. This will lower the CO_2 concentration in the tube.

control   foil   gauze   uncovered

I'll swap you 10 litres of carbon dioxide for 5 litres of methane...

This might sound like a very long-winded way of getting some different-coloured tubes, but CO_2 is pretty hard to measure (it's colourless, odourless and generally like the rest of the air), so this is actually a pretty neat way to show it.

Q1   A student puts a fresh leaf into a test tube containing orange hydrogen-carbonate indicator.
      He completely wraps the tube in foil. He leaves the tube for one hour.
      Describe and explain what you would expect the student to observe.   [3 marks]

The Respiratory System and Ventilation

You need to get oxygen into your bloodstream to supply your cells for respiration. You also need to get rid of carbon dioxide from your blood. This all happens in your lungs when you breathe air in and out.

The Lungs Are in the Thorax

1) The thorax is the top part of your body.

2) It's separated from the lower part of the body by a muscle called the diaphragm.

3) The lungs are like big pink sponges and are surrounded by the pleural membranes.

4) The lungs are protected by the ribcage. The intercostal muscles run between the ribs.

5) The air that you breathe in goes through the trachea. This splits into two tubes called bronchi (each one is a bronchus), one going to each lung.

6) The bronchi split into progressively smaller tubes called bronchioles.

7) The bronchioles finally end at small bags called alveoli where the gas exchange takes place (see page 35).

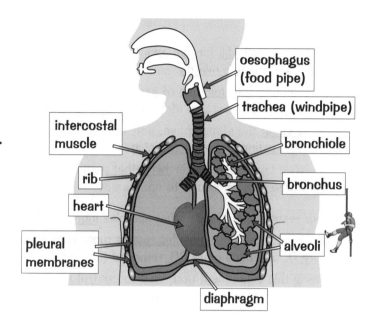

Breathing In...

1) Intercostal muscles and diaphragm contract.
2) Thorax volume increases.
3) This decreases the pressure, drawing air in.

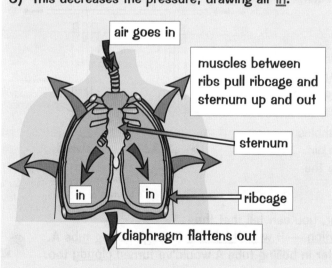

...and Breathing Out

1) Intercostal muscles and diaphragm relax.
2) Thorax volume decreases.
3) Air is forced out.

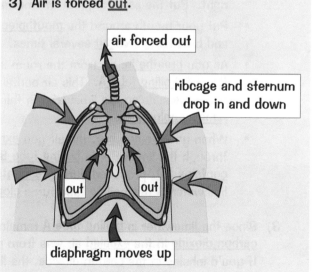

Stop huffing and puffing and just learn it...

So when you breathe in, you don't have to suck the air in. You just make the space in your lungs bigger and the air rushes in to fill it. Once you've got this page learned, flip over. And don't forget to breathe...

Q1 Explain the role of the intercostal muscles and diaphragm in ventilation. [4 marks]

Q2 Describe the passage of air from the nose and mouth to the alveoli. [3 marks]

 # Investigating Breathing

When you exercise, your muscle cells respire more — they need more O_2 and more CO_2 is produced. So an increase in your breathing rate helps to deliver more oxygen to the cells and to remove the waste CO_2.

You Can Investigate the Effect of Exercise on Breathing Rate

1) There's a really simple experiment you can do to see what happens to breathing rate when you exercise:

- Firstly, sit still for five minutes.
  Then, for one minute, count the number of breaths you take.
- Now do four minutes of exercise (running, skipping, Mexican waving...) and as soon as you stop count your breaths for a minute.
- Repeat the steps above, and work out your mean (average) results for resting and after exercise.
- You could also pester two other people to do the same so you get three sets of results to compare.

2) Your results should show that exercise increases breathing rate.

3) This is because your muscles respire more during exercise. They need to be supplied with more O_2 and have more CO_2 removed (see p.29), so your breathing rate increases.

4) During this experiment you need to control all the variables that might affect your results — e.g. you can control the time spent exercising using a stopwatch and the temperature of the room using air conditioning (ooh, fancy) or a thermostat.

You Can Investigate the Release of Carbon Dioxide in Your Breath

1) You can do an experiment with limewater to show that carbon dioxide is released when we breathe out.

2) Limewater is a colourless solution which turns cloudy in the presence of carbon dioxide.

- Set up two boiling tubes as in the diagram on the right. Put the same amount of limewater in each.
- Put your mouth around the mouthpiece and breathe in and out several times.
- As you breathe in, air from the room is drawn in through boiling tube A. This air contains very little carbon dioxide so the limewater in this boiling tube remains colourless.
- When you breathe out, the air you exhale bubbles through the limewater in boiling tube B. This air contains CO_2 produced during respiration, so the limewater in this boiling tube turns cloudy.

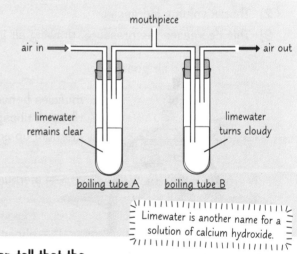

Limewater is another name for a solution of calcium hydroxide.

3) Since the limewater in boiling tube A remains clear, you can tell that the carbon dioxide in the exhaled air was from respiration — it wasn't inhaled through boiling tube A. If you'd inhaled in the carbon dioxide, the limewater in boiling tube A would've turned cloudy too.

Let's all be thankful that carbon dioxide doesn't smell like garlic...

Phew, just reading about doing exercise exhausts me. These experiments are pretty straightforward though, so learning them shouldn't be too tiring. Then once you think you've got it, take a breath and have a go at these questions.

Q1 Suggest two variables that you should control during an investigation into the effect of exercise on breathing rate. [2 marks]

Q2 A student blows through a straw into a beaker containing limewater for 15 seconds. Explain why the limewater turns cloudy. [1 mark]

Gas Exchange — Humans

Gas exchange doesn't only happen in plants — it happens in humans too.
Oxygen goes into your bloodstream and you offload nasty 'orrible carbon dioxide...

Alveoli Carry Out Gas Exchange in the Body

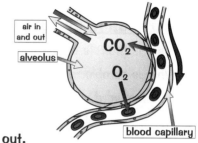

1) The lungs contain millions and millions of little air sacs called alveoli where gas exchange happens.

2) The blood passing next to the alveoli has just returned to the lungs from the rest of the body, so it contains lots of carbon dioxide and very little oxygen. Oxygen diffuses out of the alveolus (high concentration) into the blood (low concentration). Carbon dioxide diffuses out of the blood (high concentration) into the alveolus (low concentration) to be breathed out.

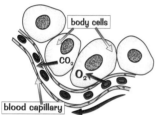

3) When the blood reaches body cells, oxygen is released from the red blood cells (where there's a high concentration) and diffuses into the body cells (where the concentration is low).

4) At the same time, carbon dioxide diffuses out of the body cells (where there's a high concentration) into the blood (where there's a low concentration). It's then carried back to the lungs.

Alveoli are Specialised for Gas Exchange

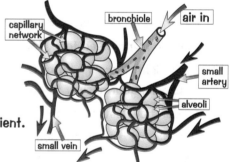

1) The huge number of microscopic alveoli gives the lungs an enormous surface area.

2) There's a moist lining for gases to dissolve in.

3) The alveoli have very thin walls — only one cell thick, so the gases don't have far to diffuse.

4) They have a great blood supply to maintain a high concentration gradient.

5) The walls are permeable — so gases can diffuse across easily.

Smoking Tobacco Can Cause Quite a Few Problems

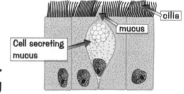

Smoking can severely affect your lungs and circulatory system. Here's how:

1) Smoking damages the walls inside the alveoli, reducing the surface area for gas exchange and leading to diseases like emphysema.

2) The tar in cigarettes damages the cilia (little hairs) in your lungs and trachea. These hairs, along with mucus, catch a load of dust and bacteria before they reach the lungs. The cilia also help to keep the trachea clear by sweeping mucus back towards the mouth. When these cilia are damaged, chest infections are more likely.

3) Tar also irritates the bronchi and bronchioles, encouraging mucus to be produced which can't be cleared very well by damaged cilia — this causes smoker's cough and chronic bronchitis.

4) The carbon monoxide in cigarette smoke reduces the amount of oxygen the blood can carry. To make up for this, heart rate increases — which leads to an increase in blood pressure. High blood pressure damages the artery walls, making the formation of blood clots more likely. This increases the risk of coronary heart disease (e.g. heart attacks).

5) Tobacco smoke also contains carcinogens — chemicals that can lead to cancer.

Alveoli — those guys are bags of fun...

The alveoli are super important in making sure that oxygen diffuses quickly enough to supply all of our cells.

Q1   Give one way in which alveoli are specialised for gas exchange.   [1 mark]

Revision Questions for Section 4

Well, that's Section 4 complete — take a deep breath and crack on with these questions.

* Try these questions and tick off each one when you get it right.
* When you've done all the questions for a topic and are completely happy with it, tick off the topic.

Respiration (p.29-30) ☑

1) What is the role of ATP?
2) What is aerobic respiration?
3) Give the word and symbol equations for aerobic respiration.
4) What is anaerobic respiration?
5) What are two drawbacks of anaerobic respiration compared to aerobic respiration?
6) Give the word equations for anaerobic respiration in:
   a) animals,
   b) plants.
7) Name an indicator solution that can be used to detect carbon dioxide.
8) Describe an experiment used to monitor the temperature change produced by respiration.

Gas Exchange — Flowering Plants (p.31-32) ☑

9) What are the little holes on the lower surface of leaves called?
10) Name the process by which plants exchange gases.
11) Why do plants need to exchange gases with their surroundings?
12) a) At night, there's a lot of O_2 inside the leaf and not a lot of CO_2. True or false?
    b) Explain your answer to part a).
13) Explain how leaves are adapted for efficient gas exchange.
14) Describe an experiment you could use to show the effect of light on gas exchange in leaves. What would you use as a control?

The Respiratory System and Ventilation (p.33-34) ☑

15) Name the key structures of the respiratory system.
16) Name the muscles that contract when you breathe in.
17) Explain why exercise increases your breathing rate.
18) Name a solution that you can use to show the presence of carbon dioxide in your breath.

Gas Exchange — Humans (p.35) ☑

19) Describe the gas exchange that happens between the alveoli and the blood.
20) Why do the alveoli have very thin walls?
21) How does smoking contribute to coronary heart disease?
22) Name two other diseases linked to smoking tobacco.

Functions of the Blood

All multicellular organisms need a transport system (see page 25) and in humans, it's the blood.

Blood has Four Main Components

They are:

| PLASMA | PLATELETS | RED BLOOD CELLS | WHITE BLOOD CELLS |

Plasma is the Liquid Bit of Blood

It's basically blood minus the blood cells (see below and on the next page). Plasma is a pale yellow liquid which carries just about everything that needs transporting around your body:

1) Red and white blood cells and platelets.
2) Digested food products (like glucose and amino acids) from the gut to all the body cells.
3) Carbon dioxide from the body cells to the lungs.
4) Urea from the liver to the kidneys (where it's removed in the urine, see page 42).
5) Hormones, which act as chemical messengers (see page 48).
6) Heat energy.

Platelets are Small Fragments of Cells that Help Blood Clot

1) When you damage a blood vessel, platelets clump together to 'plug' the damaged area.
2) This is known as blood clotting. Blood clots stop you losing too much blood and prevent microorganisms from entering the wound.
3) In a clot, platelets are held together by a mesh of a protein called fibrin (though this process also needs other proteins called clotting factors to work properly).

Red Blood Cells Have the Job of Carrying Oxygen

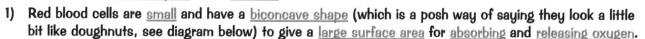

They transport oxygen from the lungs to all the cells in the body. A red blood cell is well adapted to its function:

1) Red blood cells are small and have a biconcave shape (which is a posh way of saying they look a little bit like doughnuts, see diagram below) to give a large surface area for absorbing and releasing oxygen.
2) They contain haemoglobin, which is what gives blood its colour — it contains a lot of iron. In the lungs, haemoglobin reacts with oxygen to become oxyhaemoglobin. In body tissues the reverse reaction happens to release oxygen to the cells.

3) Red blood cells don't have a nucleus — this frees up space for more haemoglobin, so they can carry more oxygen.

Blood's other function is to let you know you're bleeding...

This book's got more blood and gore than your average horror movie, but I'm afraid you're not allowed to hide behind the sofa — you need to keep your eyes open and your wits about you. By the way, if you're thinking that this book's got less humour than your average comedy, that's because the ~~best~~ rude bits get cut out.

Q1   Outline three ways in which red blood cells are adapted to carry oxygen.   [3 marks]

White Blood Cells and Immunity

Your body is <u>constantly</u> fighting off attack from all sorts of <u>nasties</u> — yep, things really are out to get you.

Your Immune System Deals with Pathogens

1) <u>Pathogens</u> are microorganisms that <u>cause disease</u>, e.g. certain types of bacteria and viruses (see p.5).

2) Once pathogens have entered your body they'll reproduce rapidly unless they're <u>destroyed</u>.
That's the job of your <u>immune system</u>, and <u>white blood cells</u> are the <u>most important part</u> of it.

3) There are two different types of white blood cell you need to know about: <u>phagocytes</u> and <u>lymphocytes</u>.

Phagocytes Ingest Pathogens

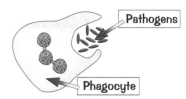

1) <u>Phagocytes</u> detect things that are 'foreign' to the body, e.g. pathogens. They then <u>engulf</u> the pathogens and <u>digest them</u>.

2) Phagocytes are <u>non-specific</u> — they attack anything that's not meant to be there.

Lymphocytes Produce Antibodies

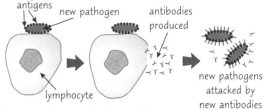

1) Every pathogen has unique molecules (called <u>antigens</u>) on its surface.

2) When certain white blood cells, called <u>lymphocytes</u>, come across a <u>foreign antigen</u>, they will start to produce <u>proteins</u> called <u>antibodies</u> — these lock on to the invading pathogens and mark them out for destruction by other white blood cells. The antibodies produced are <u>specific</u> to that type of antigen — they won't lock on to any others.

3) Antibodies are then produced <u>rapidly</u> and flow round the body to mark all similar pathogens.

4) <u>Memory cells</u> are also produced in response to a foreign antigen. These remain in the body and <u>remember</u> a <u>specific</u> antigen. They can reproduce very fast if the <u>same</u> antigen enters the body again. That's why you're <u>immune</u> to <u>most</u> diseases if you've already had them — the body carries a "memory" of what the antigen was like, and can quickly produce loads of antibodies if you get infected again.

Vaccination — Protects from Future Infections

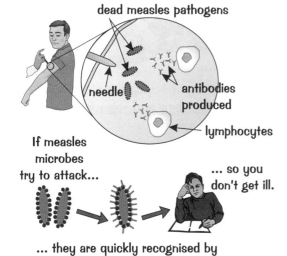

1) When you're infected with a <u>new</u> pathogen it can take your lymphocytes a while to produce the antibodies to deal with it. In that time you can get <u>very ill</u>, or maybe even die.

2) To avoid this you can be <u>vaccinated</u> against some diseases, e.g. polio or measles.

3) Vaccination usually involves injecting <u>dead or inactive</u> pathogens into the body. These carry <u>antigens</u>, so even though they're <u>harmless</u> they still trigger an <u>immune response</u> — your lymphocytes produce <u>antibodies</u> to attack them.

4) <u>Memory cells</u> will also be produced and will remain in the blood, so if <u>live</u> pathogens of the <u>same type</u> ever appear, the antibodies to <u>kill them</u> will be produced much faster and in greater numbers.

Revision questions are a lot like vaccinations...

We expose you to some harmless questions (the vaccine) that you learn how to recognise and answer, then when you're confronted with the real exam (the full strength pathogen), you've got the necessary knowledge (memory cells and antibodies) to answer (kill) them. Gosh that was a good analogy — if I may say so myself...

Q1   Outline how phagocytes defend the body against disease.   [1 mark]

Blood Vessels

Blood needs a good set of 'tubes' to carry it round the body. Here's a page on the different types:

Blood Vessels are Designed for Their Function

There are three different types of blood vessel:

1) ARTERIES — these carry the blood away from the heart.
2) CAPILLARIES — these are involved in the exchange of materials at the tissues.
3) VEINS — these carry the blood to the heart.

Arteries Carry Blood Under Pressure

1) The heart pumps the blood out at high pressure so the artery walls are strong and elastic.
2) The elastic fibres allow arteries to expand.
3) The walls are thick compared to the size of the hole down the middle (the "lumen" — silly name). They contain thick layers of muscle to make them strong.
4) The largest artery in the body is the aorta (see next page).

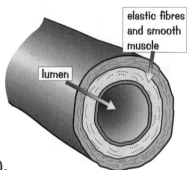

Capillaries are Really Small

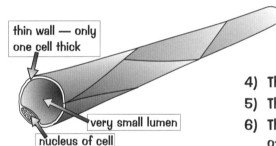

1) Arteries branch into capillaries.
2) Capillaries are really tiny — too small to see.
3) They carry the blood really close to every cell in the body to exchange substances with them.
4) They have permeable walls, so substances can diffuse in and out.
5) They supply food and oxygen, and take away wastes like CO_2.
6) Their walls are usually only one cell thick. This increases the rate of diffusion by decreasing the distance over which it happens.

Veins Take Blood Back to the Heart

1) Capillaries eventually join up to form veins.
2) The blood is at lower pressure in the veins so the walls don't need to be as thick as artery walls.
3) They have a bigger lumen than arteries to help the blood flow despite the lower pressure.
4) They also have valves to help keep the blood flowing in the right direction.
5) The largest vein in the body is the vena cava (see next page).

Learn this page — don't struggle in vein...

Here's an interesting fact for you — your body contains about 60 000 miles of blood vessels. That's about six times the distance from London to Sydney in Australia. Of course, capillaries are really tiny, which is how there can be so many miles of them inside you. They can also only be seen under a microscope.

Q1   Describe how veins are adapted to carry blood back to the heart.   [2 marks]

The Heart

Blood doesn't just move around the body on its own, of course. It needs a pump.

Learn This Diagram of the Heart with All Its Labels

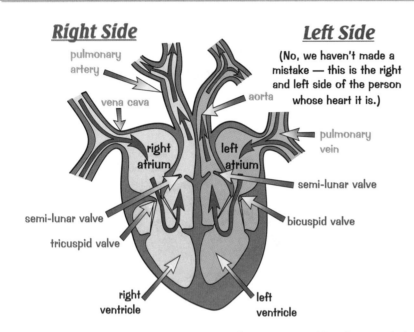

Right Side

pulmonary artery
vena cava
right atrium
semi-lunar valve
tricuspid valve
right ventricle

Left Side

(No, we haven't made a mistake — this is the right and left side of the person whose heart it is.)

aorta
pulmonary vein
semi-lunar valve
bicuspid valve
left atrium
left ventricle

1) The right atrium of the heart receives deoxygenated blood from the body (through the vena cava).
   (The plural of atrium is atria.)

2) The deoxygenated blood moves through to the right ventricle, which pumps it to the lungs (via the pulmonary artery).

3) The left atrium receives oxygenated blood from the lungs (through the pulmonary vein).

4) The oxygenated blood then moves through to the left ventricle, which pumps it out round the whole body (via the aorta).

5) The left ventricle has a much thicker wall than the right ventricle.

It needs more muscle because it has to pump blood around the whole body, whereas the right ventricle only has to pump it to the lungs. This also means that the blood in the left ventricle is under higher pressure than the blood in the right ventricle.

6) The valves prevent the backflow of blood.

Exercise Increases Heart Rate

1) When you exercise, your muscles need more energy, so you respire more.

2) You need to get more oxygen into the cells and remove more carbon dioxide. For this to happen the blood has to flow faster, so your heart rate increases. Here's how:

   There's more on respiration on p.29.

   - Exercise increases the amount of carbon dioxide in the blood.
   - High levels of blood CO_2 are detected by receptors in the aorta and carotid artery (an artery in the neck).
   - These receptors send signals to the brain.
   - The brain sends signals to the heart, causing it to contract more frequently and with more force.

The Hormonal System Also Helps to Control Heart Rate

1) When an organism is threatened (e.g. by a predator) the adrenal glands release adrenaline.

2) Adrenaline binds to specific receptors in the heart. This causes the cardiac muscle to contract more frequently and with more force, so heart rate increases and the heart pumps more blood.

3) This increases oxygen supply to the tissues, getting the body ready for action.

I ♥ revising...

If you were expecting a smooshy, soppy page about feelings and relationships, I'm sorry to disappoint. You've got to know the inside of your heart like the back of your hand. If you don't bother learning this page, you'll feel pretty silly if you turn over the exam paper and the first question asks you to label a diagram of the heart.

Q1   Explain the effect of adrenaline on heart rate.   [3 marks]

Circulation and Coronary Heart Disease

The circulation system is made up of the heart and the blood vessels. It's responsible for getting the blood to where it needs to be, so that useful substances (e.g. glucose and oxygen) can be delivered and wastes removed.

You Need to Know the Structure of the Circulation System

The diagram below shows the human circulation system.

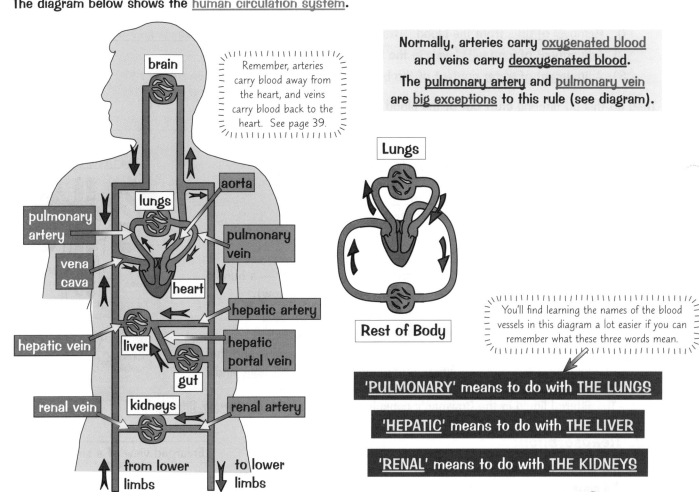

Remember, arteries carry blood away from the heart, and veins carry blood back to the heart. See page 39.

Normally, arteries carry oxygenated blood and veins carry deoxygenated blood.

The pulmonary artery and pulmonary vein are big exceptions to this rule (see diagram).

You'll find learning the names of the blood vessels in this diagram a lot easier if you can remember what these three words mean.

'PULMONARY' means to do with THE LUNGS

'HEPATIC' means to do with THE LIVER

'RENAL' means to do with THE KIDNEYS

Several Factors can Lead to Coronary Heart Disease

1) Coronary heart disease is when the coronary arteries that supply the blood to the muscle of the heart get blocked by layers of fatty material building up.

2) This causes the arteries to become narrow, so blood flow is restricted and there's a lack of oxygen to the heart muscle — this can lead to a heart attack.

3) There are many risk factors for coronary heart disease. Risk factors are things that are linked to an increase in the likelihood that a person will develop a certain disease during their lifetime.

4) One risk factor for coronary heart disease is having a diet high in saturated fat. This can lead to fatty deposits forming inside arteries, which can lead to coronary heart disease.

5) Smoking is another risk factor for coronary heart disease. Smoking increases blood pressure, which can cause damage to the inside of the coronary arteries. Chemicals in cigarette smoke can also cause damage. The damage makes it more likely that fatty deposits will form, narrowing the coronary arteries.

6) Another risk factor for coronary heart disease is being inactive. It can lead to high blood pressure, which can damage the lining of arteries. This damage makes it more likely that fatty deposits will form.

The circulation system — named after Sir Q. Lation in 1821...

You need to know the circulation system in a fair bit of detail so don't move on until you've got to grips with it.

Q1   Name the vessel that takes blood away from the kidneys.   [1 mark]

Excretion — The Kidneys

Excretion is the removal of waste products. Carbon dioxide is a waste product from the lungs, and sweat is a waste product from the skin. Excretion is also carried out by the kidneys.

The Kidneys are Excretion Organs

The kidneys are part of the urinary system. They perform three main roles:

1) Removal of urea from the blood. Urea is produced in the liver from excess amino acids.
2) Adjustment of ion (salt) levels in the blood.
3) Adjustment of water content of the blood.

They do this by filtering stuff out of the blood under high pressure, and then reabsorbing the useful things. The end product is urine.

So the excretory products of the kidney are urea, ions and water.

Nephrons are the Filtration Units in the Kidneys

Each kidney contains thousands of nephrons.
Here's what happens as the blood passes through them:

1. Ultrafiltration:

1) Blood from the renal artery flows through the glomerulus — a bundle of capillaries at the start of the nephron (see diagram below).
2) A high pressure is built up which squeezes water, urea, ions and glucose out of the blood and into the Bowman's capsule.
3) The membranes between the blood vessels in the glomerulus and the Bowman's capsule act like filters, so big molecules like proteins and blood cells are not squeezed out. They stay in the blood. The filtered liquid in the Bowman's capsule is known as the glomerular filtrate.

2. Reabsorption:

As the filtrate flows along the nephron, useful substances are selectively reabsorbed back into the blood:

1) All the glucose is reabsorbed from the proximal convoluted tubule so that it can be used in respiration. The reabsorption of glucose involves the process of active transport (see p.11) against the concentration gradient.
2) Sufficient ions are reabsorbed. Excess ions aren't.
3) Sufficient water is reabsorbed from the collecting duct into the bloodstream by osmosis (see p.9).

It's called selective reabsorption because only some substances are reabsorbed.

3. Release of Wastes:

The remaining substances (including water, ions and urea) form urine. This continues out of the nephron, through the ureter and down to the bladder, where it is stored before being released via the urethra.

The Urinary System

Enlarged view of a single nephron

Filtration happens here.
glomerulus
capillary network
blood from renal artery
Bowman's capsule
proximal convoluted tubule
Reabsorption happens here, as does water regulation.
blood to renal vein
from another nephron
distal convoluted tubule
collecting duct
loop of Henle
Release of wastes.
urine

KEY:
= blood   → = reabsorption
= fluid in nephron   ⇢ = filtration

Removal of urea — nothing to do with Vincent van Gogh...

There's lots to learn here, but it's broken down into nice chunks — so just take them one by one and all will be fine...

Q1   Give two excretory products of the kidneys.   [2 marks]

Osmoregulation — The Kidneys

The kidneys are <u>really important</u> organs. Not only do they filter the blood (see previous page), they also play a key role in controlling the amount of water inside your body. Whether you're interested in it or not, I'm afraid <u>you need to know this page</u> for your exam — so <u>pay attention</u>.

The Kidneys Also Adjust the Body's Water Content

1) Water is taken into the body as <u>food and drink</u> and is <u>lost</u> from the body in <u>three main ways</u>: sweating, breathing and weeing (see page 49).

2) The body has to <u>constantly balance</u> the water coming <u>in</u> against the water going <u>out</u> — this is <u>osmoregulation</u>.

3) One way that it can do this is by adjusting the amount of water that is <u>excreted by the kidneys</u> in the <u>urine</u>. E.g. If a person is <u>sweating</u> a lot or hasn't <u>drunk</u> enough water, the kidneys can reabsorb more water (see below), so that less is <u>lost in the urine</u> and the water balance is <u>maintained</u>.

4) When the kidneys reabsorb more water, the urine has a <u>smaller volume</u> and is <u>more concentrated</u>.

ADH Helps to Control Water Content

1) The amount of water reabsorbed in the kidney nephrons is <u>controlled</u> by a hormone called <u>anti-diuretic hormone</u> (ADH). ADH makes the collecting ducts of the nephrons <u>more permeable</u> so more water is <u>reabsorbed</u> back into the blood.

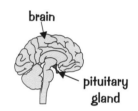

brain

pituitary gland

2) The brain <u>monitors the water content of the blood</u> and instructs the <u>pituitary gland</u> to release <u>ADH</u> into the blood according to how much is needed.

3) The whole process of osmoregulation is controlled by a mechanism called <u>negative feedback</u>. This means that if the water content gets <u>too high</u> or <u>too low</u> a mechanism will be triggered that brings it back to <u>normal</u>.

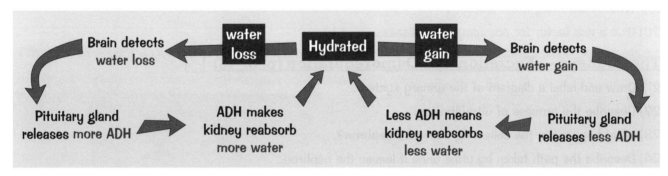

Don't try to kid-me that you know it all — learn it properly...

So the kidneys make sure you don't end up like a dry sponge or a massive water balloon — thank goodness. Make sure you remember which way round ADH works. Basically, low blood water content means increased ADH production and more water reabsorbed in the kidneys. High blood water content means decreased ADH production and less water reabsorbed. What could be simpler... erm, actually, let's not get started on that.

Q1   Give three ways that water is lost from the body.   [3 marks]

Q2   Explain how an increase in the release of ADH helps to regulate the water content of the blood when the brain detects that it is too low.   [2 marks]

Revision Questions for Section 5

Well, Section 5 has been a ball. You know what it's time for...

- Try these questions and tick off each one when you get it right.
- When you've done all the questions for a topic and are completely happy with it, tick off the topic.

Functions of the Blood, White Blood Cells and Immunity (p.37-38) ☑

1) What are the four main components of blood?
2) Name six things that blood plasma transports around the body.
3) What are platelets? What role do they play in the body?
4) Describe the shape of a red blood cell.
5) How do lymphocytes defend the body from pathogens?
6) Explain the role of memory cells in the immune system's response against pathogens.
7) Explain how vaccination prevents you from getting a particular infection.

Blood Vessels and The Heart (p.39-40) ☐

8) Why do arteries need very muscular, elastic walls?
9) Explain how capillaries are adapted to their function.
10) Which blood vessels have valves?
11) Draw and label a simple diagram of the heart.
12) Name the blood vessel that joins to the right ventricle of the heart. Where does it take the blood?
13) Why does the left ventricle have a thicker wall than the right ventricle?
14) How does heart rate change during exercise? Why?
15) What hormone causes heart rate to rise?

Circulation and Coronary Heart Disease (p.41) ☐

16) What is the name of the blood vessel that carries blood away from the liver?
17) What is the function of the renal artery?
18) What are the names of the two main blood vessels associated with the lungs?
19) What is coronary heart disease?
20) Give a risk factor for coronary heart disease.

The Kidneys — Excretion and Osmoregulation (p.42-43) ☑

21) Draw and label a diagram of the urinary system.
22) Describe the process of ultrafiltration.
23) What happens in the collecting duct of a nephron?
24) Describe the path taken by urine once it leaves the nephron.
25) Which hormone is responsible for controlling the amount of water reabsorbed in the kidneys?

The Nervous System and Responding to Stimuli

Right, it's time to get your brain cells fired up and take a hit of adrenaline — this section's a corker.

Responding to Their Environment Helps Organisms Survive

1) Animals increase their chances of survival by responding to changes in their external environment, e.g. by avoiding places that are too hot or too cold.

2) They also respond to changes in their internal environment to make sure that the conditions are always right for their metabolism (all the chemical reactions that go on inside them).

3) Plants also increase their chances of survival by responding to changes in their environment (see page 51).

4) Any change in the internal or external environment is called a stimulus.

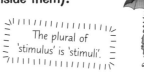 The plural of 'stimulus' is 'stimuli'.

Receptors Detect Stimuli and Effectors Produce a Response

1) Receptors detect stimuli. Receptors in the sense organs (the eyes, ears, nose, tongue and skin) are groups of cells that detect external stimuli. E.g. rod and cone cells in the eye detect changes in light (see page 47).

2) Effectors are cells that bring about a response to stimuli. They include muscle cells and cells found in glands, e.g. the pancreas. Effectors respond in different ways — muscle cells contract, whereas glands secrete hormones.

3) Receptors communicate with effectors via the nervous system (see below), the hormonal system (see page 48) or sometimes both.

The Central Nervous System (CNS) Coordinates Information

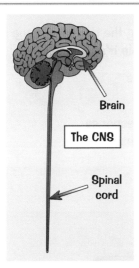

Brain

The CNS

Spinal cord

1) The nervous system is made up of all the neurones (nerve cells) in your body. There are three main types of neurone — sensory neurones, relay neurones and motor neurones.

2) The central nervous system (CNS) consists of the brain and spinal cord only.

3) When receptors in a sense organ detect a stimulus, they send electrical impulses along sensory neurones to the CNS.

4) The CNS then sends electrical impulses to an effector along a motor neurone. The effector then responds accordingly.

5) The job of the CNS is to coordinate the response. Coordinated responses always need a stimulus, a receptor and an effector.

6) Because neurones transmit information using high speed electrical impulses, the nervous system is able to bring about very rapid responses.

Synapses Connect Neurones

1) The connection between two neurones is called a synapse.

2) The nerve signal is transferred by chemicals called neurotransmitters which diffuse (move) across the gap.

3) These chemicals then set off a new electrical signal in the next neurone.

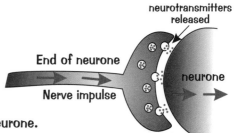
neurotransmitters released
End of neurone
Nerve impulse
neurone

If only my broadband was as fast as the CNS...

So without receptors, neurones and effectors you wouldn't be able to respond to your environment. Sad times.

Q1   Name the two main parts of the central nervous system.   [2 marks]

Reflexes

Your brain can <u>decide</u> how to respond to a stimulus <u>pretty quickly</u>. But sometimes waiting for your brain to make a decision is just <u>too slow</u>. That's why you have <u>reflexes</u>.

Reflexes Help Prevent Injury

1) <u>Reflexes</u> are <u>automatic</u> responses to certain stimuli — they can reduce the chances of being injured.

2) For example, if someone shines a <u>bright light</u> in your eyes, your <u>pupils</u> automatically get smaller so that less light gets into the eyes — this stops them getting <u>damaged</u> (see next page).

3) Or if you get a shock, your body releases the <u>hormone</u> adrenaline automatically — it doesn't wait for you to <u>decide</u> that you're shocked.

4) The route taken by the information in a reflex (from receptor to effector) is called a <u>reflex arc</u>.

The Reflex Arc Goes Through the Central Nervous System

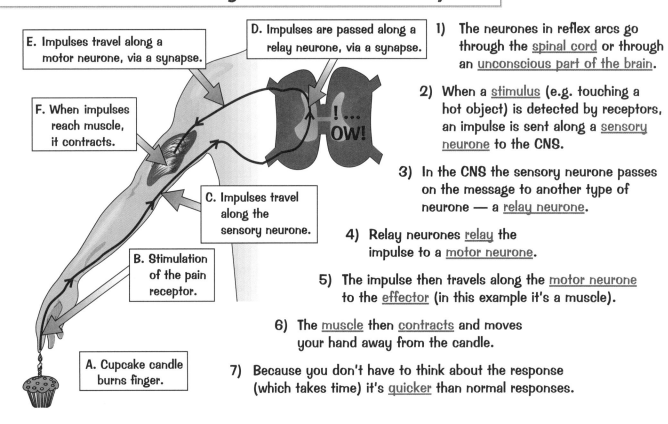

E. Impulses travel along a motor neurone, via a synapse.

D. Impulses are passed along a relay neurone, via a synapse.

F. When impulses reach muscle, it contracts.

C. Impulses travel along the sensory neurone.

B. Stimulation of the pain receptor.

A. Cupcake candle burns finger.

1) The neurones in reflex arcs go through the <u>spinal cord</u> or through an <u>unconscious part of the brain</u>.

2) When a <u>stimulus</u> (e.g. touching a hot object) is detected by receptors, an impulse is sent along a <u>sensory neurone</u> to the CNS.

3) In the CNS the sensory neurone passes on the message to another type of neurone — a <u>relay neurone</u>.

4) Relay neurones <u>relay</u> the impulse to a <u>motor neurone</u>.

5) The impulse then travels along the <u>motor neurone</u> to the <u>effector</u> (in this example it's a muscle).

6) The <u>muscle</u> then <u>contracts</u> and moves your hand away from the candle.

7) Because you don't have to think about the response (which takes time) it's <u>quicker</u> than normal responses.

You Can Draw a Block Diagram to Represent a Reflex Arc

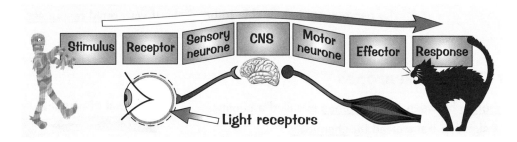

Stimulus | Receptor | Sensory neurone | CNS | Motor neurone | Effector | Response

Light receptors

Reflex — but only if she hasn't noticed how muscly you are already...

Remember that reflex arcs don't involve the conscious part of the central nervous system — so there's no time wasted while you mess about making a decision. This is what makes them super fast and highly effective.

Q1   A chef touches a hot tray. A reflex reaction causes him to immediately move his hand away.
Describe the pathway of the reflex arc from receptors to effector.   [4 marks]

The Eye

The eye is a good example of a sense organ, and there are several parts you need to learn about.

Learn the Eye with All Its Labels

1) The CONJUNCTIVA lubricates and protects the surface of the eye.

2) The SCLERA is the tough outer layer that protects the eye.

3) The CORNEA refracts (bends) light into the eye. The cornea is transparent and has no blood vessels to supply it with oxygen, so oxygen diffuses in from the outer surface.

4) The IRIS controls the diameter of the PUPIL (the hole in the middle) and therefore how much light enters the eye.

5) The LENS focuses the light onto the RETINA (the light-sensitive part — it's covered in light receptors called rods and cones).
Rods are more sensitive in dim light but can't sense colour. Cones are sensitive to colours but aren't so good in dim light. Cones are found all over the retina, but there are loads of them at the FOVEA.

5) The OPTIC NERVE carries impulses from the receptors to the brain.

The Iris Reflex — Adjusting for Bright Light

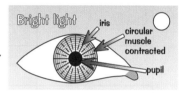

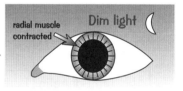

Very bright light can damage the retina — so you have a reflex to protect it.

1) Very bright light triggers a reflex that makes the pupil smaller, allowing less light in. (See the previous page for more about reflexes... but basically, in this case, light receptors detect the bright light and send a message along a sensory neurone to the brain. The message then travels along a relay neurone to a motor neurone, which tells circular muscles in the iris to contract, making the pupil smaller.)

2) The opposite process happens in dim light. This time, the brain tells the radial muscles to contract, which makes the pupil bigger.

Focusing on Near and Distant Objects — Another Reflex

The eye focuses light on the retina by changing the shape of the lens — this is known as accommodation.

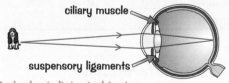

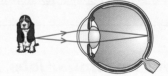

As you get older, your eye's lens loses flexibility, so it can't easily spring back to a round shape. This means light can't be focused well for near viewing, so older people often have to use reading glasses.

To look at distant objects:
1) The ciliary muscles relax, which allows the suspensory ligaments to pull tight.
2) This makes the lens go thin (less curved).
3) So it refracts light by a smaller amount.

To look at near objects:
1) The ciliary muscles contract, which slackens the suspensory ligaments.
2) The lens becomes fat (more curved).
3) This increases the amount by which it refracts light.

1) Short-sighted people are unable to focus on distant objects. This occurs when the cornea or lens bends the light too much or the eyeball is too long. The images of distant objects are brought into focus in front of the retina.

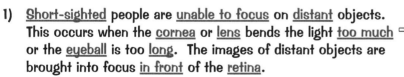

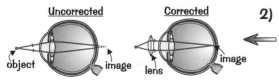

2) Long-sighted people are unable to focus on near objects. This occurs when the cornea or lens doesn't bend the light enough or the eyeball is too short. The images of near objects are brought into focus behind the retina.

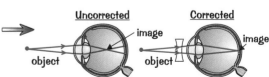

Eye eye, Captain...

It doesn't matter how good you are at blagging in the exam — you need to learn those diagrams of the eye.

Q1   Explain how the eye focuses on an object that's close to it.   [4 marks]

Hormones

The other way to send information around the body (apart from along nerves) is by using hormones.

Hormones Are Chemical Messengers Sent in the Blood

1) Hormones are chemicals released directly into the blood. They're carried in the blood plasma to other parts of the body, but only affect particular cells (called target cells) in particular places. Hormones control things in organs and cells that need constant adjustment.

2) Hormones are produced in glands. They travel quite slowly and tend to have relatively long-lasting effects.

Each Different Hormone in the Body has its Own Job

You need to know where each of these hormones is made and what they do.

Hormone	Source	Role	Effects
Adrenaline	Adrenal glands (on top of the kidneys)	Readies the body for a 'fight or flight' response (see below).	Increases heart rate, blood flow to muscles and blood sugar level.
Insulin	Pancreas	Helps control the blood sugar level.	Stimulates the liver to turn glucose into glycogen for storage.
Testosterone	Testes	Main male sex hormone.	Promotes male secondary sexual characteristics, e.g. facial hair (see p.62).
Progesterone	Ovaries	Supports pregnancy.	Maintains the lining of the uterus (see p.63).
Oestrogen	Ovaries	Main female sex hormone.	Controls the menstrual cycle and promotes female secondary sexual characteristics, e.g. widening of the hips (see p.62 and 63).
ADH (anti-diuretic hormone)	Pituitary gland (in the brain)	Controls water content.	Increases the permeability of the kidney tubules to water (see p.43).
FSH	Pituitary gland	Female sex hormone.	Causes an egg to mature in an ovary. Stimulates the ovaries to produce oestrogen.
LH	Pituitary gland	Female sex hormone.	Stimulates the release of an egg from an ovary.

Hormones and Nerves Do Similar Jobs, but There Are Differences

NERVES: 1) Very FAST message. 2) Act for a very SHORT TIME. 3) Act on a very PRECISE AREA.

HORMONES: 1) SLOWER message. 2) Act for a LONG TIME. 3) Act in a more GENERAL way.

So if you're not sure whether a response is nervous or hormonal, have a think...

1) If the response is really quick, it's probably nervous.
2) Some information needs to be passed to effectors really quickly (e.g. pain signals, or information from your eyes telling you about the lion heading your way).
3) It's no good using hormones to carry the message — they're too slow.
4) But if a response lasts for a long time, it's probably hormonal.
5) For example, when you get a shock, a hormone called adrenaline is released into the bloodstream (causing the fight-or-flight response, where your body is hyped up ready for action).

Testes — not quite as bad as examies...

Hormones control various organs and cells in the body. Their effects also tend to be fairly long lasting.

Q1 Where in the body is the source of oestrogen? [1 mark]

Homeostasis

Homeostasis involves balancing body functions to maintain a "constant internal environment".
Hormones are sometimes (but not always) involved.

Homeostasis — it's all about Balance

Conditions in your body need to be kept steady so that cells can function properly. This involves
balancing inputs (stuff going into your body) with outputs (stuff leaving). For example...

Water content — you need to keep a balance between
the water you gain and the water you lose (see below).

Body temperature — you need to get rid of excess body heat
when you're hot, but retain heat when the environment is cold.

Homeostasis is what keeps these conditions balanced. Don't forget:

> Homeostasis is the maintenance of a constant internal environment.

Water is Lost from the Body in Various Ways

Water is taken into the body as food and drink and is lost from the body in the following ways:

1) through the skin as sweat...
2) via the lungs in breath...
3) via the kidneys as urine.

Some water is also lost in faeces.

The balance between sweat and urine can depend on what you're doing, or what the weather's like...

- On a hot day, or when you're exercising, you sweat a lot.
- You will produce less urine, but this will be more concentrated (and hence a deeper colour).
- You will also lose more water through your breath when you exercise because you breathe faster.

- On a cold day, or when you're not exercising, you don't sweat much.
- You'll produce more urine, which will be pale (since the waste carried in the urine is more diluted).

Body Temperature is Kept at About 37 °C

1) All enzymes work best at a certain optimum temperature (see page 6).
   The enzymes in the human body work best at about 37 °C — and so
   this is the temperature your body tries to maintain.
2) A part of the brain acts as your own personal thermostat. It's sensitive to the blood
   temperature in the brain, and it receives messages from temperature receptors in the
   skin that provide information about skin temperature.
3) Based on the signals from these receptors, your central nervous system can activate
   the necessary effectors to make sure your body temperature stays just right.

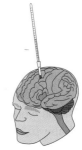

I've just had a huge glass of water — I'm going to time homeostasis...

As you're reading this book, your body is checking the levels of all sorts of variables and tweaking them so that the
conditions are spot on for your body's enzymes to work perfectly. If this wasn't happening, you'd be in real trouble.
It's a delicate balance, but luckily you don't have to concentrate on it — your body does it all for you.

Q1   A runner is running a race on a hot day, and only drinks a small amount of water.
Suggest why his urine will be concentrated.

[2 marks]

More on Homeostasis

Homeostasis is so <u>important</u> for organisms (and for science students) that I just couldn't <u>resist</u> writing a second page on it for you. If you <u>enjoy</u> reading it half as much as I enjoyed writing it — you're in for a <u>treat</u>.

The Skin Plays an Important Role in Maintaining Body Temperature

To <u>stay</u> at a <u>cosy-but-not-too-warm</u> **37 °C** your body has a few <u>tricks</u> up its sleeve:

When You're Too Hot:

1) <u>Lots of sweat</u> is produced — when it <u>evaporates</u> it <u>transfers energy</u> from your skin to the environment, cooling you down.
2) <u>Blood vessels</u> close to the surface of the skin <u>widen</u> — this is called <u>vasodilation</u>. It allows more blood to flow near the surface, so it can <u>transfer more energy</u> into the <u>surroundings</u>, which cools you down.
3) <u>Hairs</u> lie flat.

When You're Too Cold:

1) <u>Very little sweat</u> is produced.
2) <u>Blood vessels</u> near the surface of the skin <u>constrict</u> (<u>vasoconstriction</u>). This means <u>less blood</u> flows near the surface, so <u>less energy</u> is transferred to the surroundings.
3) You <u>shiver</u>, which increases your rate of <u>respiration</u>, which transfers more <u>energy</u> to <u>warm</u> the body. <u>Exercise</u> does the same.
4) <u>Hairs</u> stand on end to trap an insulating layer of air, which helps keep you warm.

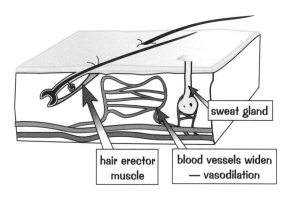

sweat gland

hair erector muscle

blood vessels widen — vasodilation

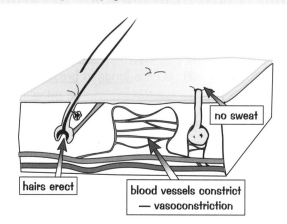

no sweat

hairs erect

blood vessels constrict — vasoconstriction

Smaller Organisms Can Cool Down Quicker

1) <u>Smaller organisms</u> have <u>bigger surface area to volume ratios</u> (see page 11).
2) Organisms with bigger surface area to volume ratios can <u>gain</u> (or <u>lose</u>) <u>heat faster</u> because there is <u>more area</u> for the heat to transfer across.
3) This allows <u>small organisms</u> to lose body heat more easily in <u>hot climates</u> and reduces the chance of them <u>overheating</u>. It also means that they're very <u>vulnerable</u> in <u>cold environments</u>.
4) Organisms with <u>smaller</u> surface area to volume ratios <u>gain</u> (or <u>lose</u>) <u>heat</u> <u>more slowly</u> because there is <u>less area</u> for the heat to transfer across.
5) This is why animals living in <u>cold</u> conditions have a <u>compact</u> (rounded) shape to keep their <u>surface area</u> to a minimum, <u>reducing heat loss</u>.

O homeo_(stasis), homeo_(stasis)! Wherefore art thou homeo_(stasis)?...

So that's why elephants have big ears — to increase their surface area to volume ratios and help them cool down quicker. You learn something new everyday, eh. Which is lucky, what with your exams and everything.

Q1   The body responds to the temperature of the external environment.
    a) Explain how the blood flow through the skin is affected when a person is too cold. [2 marks]
    b) Give another way that the skin responds when a person is too cold. [1 mark]

Responses in Plants

You're <u>nearly</u> done for this section. Just this <u>little bit</u> about plants still to go — they're just as important...

Plants Need to Respond to Stimuli Too

1) Plants, like animals, <u>increase</u> their chances of <u>survival</u> by responding to changes in their environment, e.g.:

   - They sense the direction of <u>light</u> and <u>grow</u> towards it to <u>maximise</u> light absorption for <u>photosynthesis</u>.
   - They can sense <u>gravity</u>, so their roots and shoots <u>grow</u> in the <u>right direction</u>.
   - <u>Climbing</u> plants have a sense of <u>touch</u>, so they can find things to climb and <u>reach</u> the <u>sunlight</u>.

2) Plants are more likely to survive if they respond to the presence of <u>predators</u> to avoid being eaten, e.g.:

   <u>White clover</u> is a plant that can produce substances that are <u>toxic</u> to <u>cattle</u>. Cattle start to <u>eat</u> lots of white clover when fields are <u>overgrazed</u> — the white clover <u>responds</u> by <u>producing toxins</u>, to <u>avoid</u> being <u>eaten</u>.

3) Plants are more likely to survive if they respond to <u>abiotic stress</u> — anything harmful that's natural but non-living, like a drought, e.g.:

   <u>Carrots</u> produce <u>antifreeze proteins</u> at low temperatures — the proteins <u>bind</u> to <u>ice crystals</u> and <u>lower</u> the <u>temperature</u> that water <u>freezes</u> at, <u>stopping</u> more ice crystals from <u>growing</u>.

Auxins are Plant Growth Hormones

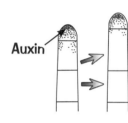

1) <u>Auxins</u> are <u>plant hormones</u> which control <u>growth</u> at the <u>tips</u> of <u>shoots</u> and <u>roots</u>. They move through the plant in <u>solution</u> (dissolved in water).

Auxin

2) Auxin is produced in the <u>tips</u> and <u>diffuses backwards</u> to stimulate the <u>cell elongation process</u> which occurs in the cells <u>just behind</u> the tips.

3) Auxin <u>promotes</u> growth in the <u>shoot</u>, but actually <u>inhibits</u> growth in the <u>root</u>.

4) Auxins are involved in the <u>growth</u> responses of plants to <u>light</u> (phototropism) and <u>gravity</u> (geotropism).

Auxins Change the Direction of Root and Shoot Growth

<u>SHOOTS ARE POSITIVELY PHOTOTROPIC (grow towards light)</u>

1) When a <u>shoot tip</u> is exposed to <u>light</u>, it accumulates <u>more auxin</u> on the side that's in the <u>shade</u> than the side that's in the light.

2) This makes the cells grow (elongate) <u>faster</u> on the <u>shaded side</u>, so the shoot bends <u>towards</u> the light.

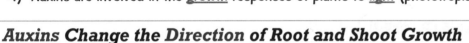

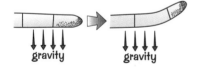

gravity   gravity

<u>SHOOTS ARE NEGATIVELY GEOTROPIC (grow away from gravity)</u>

1) When a <u>shoot</u> is growing sideways, <u>gravity</u> produces an unequal distribution of auxin in the tip, with <u>more auxin</u> on the <u>lower side</u>.

2) This causes the lower side to grow <u>faster</u>, bending the shoot <u>upwards</u>.

<u>ROOTS ARE POSITIVELY GEOTROPIC (grow towards gravity)</u>

1) A <u>root</u> growing sideways will also have more auxin on its <u>lower side</u>.

2) But in a root the <u>extra</u> auxin <u>inhibits</u> growth. This means the cells on <u>top</u> elongate faster, and the root bends <u>downwards</u>.

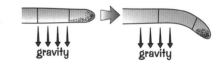

gravity   gravity

<u>ROOTS ARE NEGATIVELY PHOTOTROPIC (grow away from light)</u>

1) If a <u>root</u> starts being exposed to some <u>light</u>, <u>more auxin</u> accumulates on the more <u>shaded</u> side.

2) The auxin <u>inhibits</u> cell elongation on the shaded side, so the root bends <u>downwards</u>, back into the ground.

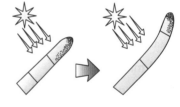

light   light

surface

Roots that are underground <u>aren't exposed</u> to light. They grow downwards due to <u>positive gravitropism</u>.

A plant auxin to a bar — 'ouch'...

Quite a bit to learn on this page — cover it up and scribble it all down till you're confident you know it all.

Q1   Explain what causes plant shoots to grow towards light.   [2 marks]

Revision Questions for Section 6

So that was <u>Section 6</u>. Not too bad, if you ask me. Before you start on Section 7, have a bash at the questions.

*   Try these questions and <u>tick off each one</u> when you <u>get it right</u>.
*   When you've done <u>all the questions</u> for a topic and are <u>completely happy</u> with it, tick off the topic.

The Nervous System, Responding to Stimuli and Reflexes (p.45-46) ☐

1) Why do organisms respond to changes in their environment?
2) What is a stimulus? How are stimuli detected?
3) Give two types of effector.
4) What does the central nervous system do?
5) What is the purpose of a reflex action?
6) Describe the pathway of a reflex arc from stimulus to response.

The Eye (p.47) ☐

7) Draw a labelled diagram of a human eye.
8) Explain the roles of the following parts of the eye:
    a) cornea
    b) iris
    c) lens
9) Describe the iris reflex. Why is this needed?
10) How does accommodation of the eye work? Is the lens fat or thin when looking at distant objects?

Hormones and Homeostasis (p.48-50) ☐

11) Define the term 'hormone'.
12) What is the role of the hormone adrenaline? What effects does it have on the body?
13) Where is insulin made? Describe insulin's role in the body.
14) Where is FSH made?
15) Describe the role of LH in the body.
16) List three differences between nervous and hormonal responses.
17) Write down two conditions that the body needs to keep fairly constant.
18) Define homeostasis.
19) Give three ways in which water is lost from the body.
20) Describe how the amount and concentration of urine you produce varies depending on how much exercise you do and how hot it is.
21) At what temperature do most of the enzymes in the human body work best?
22) Describe how body temperature is reduced when you're too hot.
23) Do smaller animals tend to have small or large surface area to volume ratios? How does this affect their temperature control?

Responses in Plants (p.51) ☐

24) Give two ways in which plants respond to stimuli.
25) What are auxins?
26) What is: a) positive phototropism?   b) positive geotropism?
27) Shoots are negatively geotropic. How are auxins responsible for this?

DNA, Genes and Chromosomes

This page is a little bit tricky, so take your time. It's dead important you get to grips with all this stuff — you're going to need it to understand the rest of the section properly...

Chromosomes are Found in the Nucleus

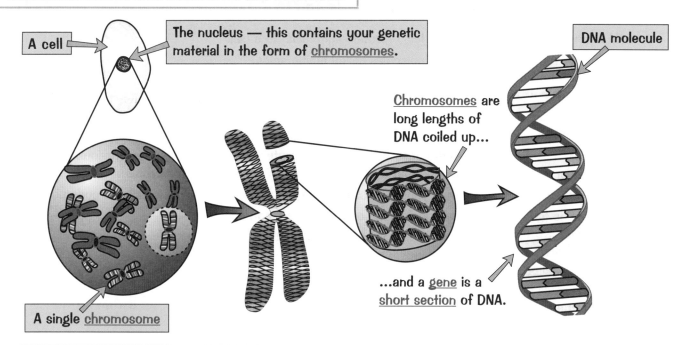

A cell

The nucleus — this contains your genetic material in the form of chromosomes.

DNA molecule

Chromosomes are long lengths of DNA coiled up...

...and a gene is a short section of DNA.

A single chromosome

Human body cells are diploid — this means they have two copies of each chromosome, arranged in pairs. A human cell nucleus contains 46 chromosomes in total — so the diploid number for a human is 46.

Genes are Chemical Instructions

1) DNA is a long list of instructions on how to put an organism together and make it work.

2) All of an organism's DNA makes up the organism's genome.

3) Each separate gene in a DNA molecule is a chemical instruction that codes for (says how to make) a particular protein.

4) Proteins are important because they control most processes in the body. They also determine inherited characteristics, e.g. eye colour, blood type.

5) By controlling the production of proteins, genes also control our inherited characteristics.

6) There can be different versions of the same gene, which give different versions of a characteristic — like blue or brown eyes. The different versions of the same gene are called alleles.

DNA is a Double Helix

1) A DNA molecule has two strands coiled together in the shape of a double helix (two spirals).

2) The two strands are held together by chemicals called bases. There are four different bases (shown in the diagram as different colours) — adenine (A), cytosine (C), guanine (G) and thymine (T).

3) The bases are paired, and they always pair up in the same way — it's always A-T and C-G. This is called complementary base-pairing.

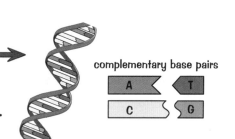

complementary base pairs

A — T
C — G

Paper 2

Insert joke about genes and jeans here...

Genes are important because they control what characteristics parents pass on to their kids. It's all to do with proteins — genes control the proteins that are made, and proteins control most processes in the body.

Q1 What is a gene? [2 marks]

Protein Synthesis

So here's how <u>life</u> works — <u>DNA molecules</u> contain a <u>genetic code</u> that determines which <u>proteins</u> are built. The proteins determine how all the <u>cells</u> in the body <u>function</u>. Simple, eh.

Proteins are Made by Reading the Code in DNA

1) DNA controls the <u>production of proteins</u> (protein synthesis) in a cell.

2) Proteins are made up of chains of molecules called <u>amino acids</u>. Each different protein has its own particular <u>number</u> and <u>order</u> of amino acids.

3) The amino acid chains <u>fold up</u> to give each protein a <u>different</u>, <u>specific shape</u> — which means each protein can have a <u>different function</u>. This is why <u>enzymes</u> have active sites with a specific shape, and so only catalyse a specific reaction (see page 6).

4) Remember, a section of DNA that codes for a <u>particular protein</u> is called a <u>gene</u> (see previous page). It's the <u>order</u> of the <u>bases</u> in a gene that decides the <u>order</u> of <u>amino acids</u> in a protein.

5) Each amino acid is coded for by a sequence of <u>three bases</u> in the gene — this is called a <u>codon</u>.

6) DNA contains <u>four</u> different bases and each codon in a gene contains <u>three</u> bases. So there are 4 × 4 × 4 = <u>64 possible codons</u>. Since there are only 20 amino acids, some codons code for the <u>same amino acid</u>.

```
AAA ACA AGA ATA CAA CCA CGA CTA
AAC ACC AGC ATC CAC CCC CGC CTC
AAG ACG AGG ATG CAG CCG CGG CTG
AAT ACT AGT ATT CAT CCT CGT CTT
GAA GCA GGA GTA TAA TCA TGA TTA
GAC GCC GGC GTC TAC TCC TGC TTC
GAG GCG GGG GTG TAG TCG TGG TTG
GAT GCT GGT GTT TAT TCT TGT TTT
```

Codons are also known as base triplets.

7) The amino acids are <u>joined together</u> to make proteins, following the order of the bases in the gene.

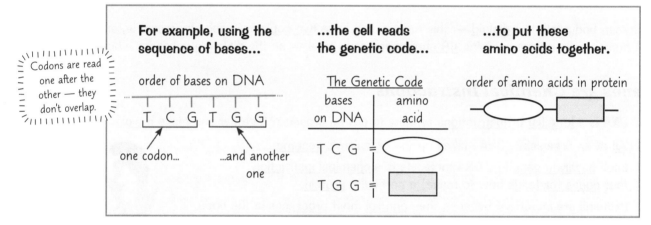

Codons are read one after the other — they don't overlap.

For example, using the sequence of bases...

order of bases on DNA

... T C G T G G ...

one codon... ...and another one

...the cell reads the genetic code...

The Genetic Code

bases on DNA	amino acid
T C G =	⬭
T G G =	▭

...to put these amino acids together.

order of amino acids in protein

8) Each gene contains a <u>different sequence</u> of bases — which is what allows it to code for a <u>particular protein</u>.

DNA Also Contains Non-Coding Regions

1) Many regions of DNA are <u>non-coding</u> — that means that they <u>don't code</u> for any <u>amino acids</u>.

2) Despite this, some of these regions are still involved in <u>protein synthesis</u> (see next page).

A triplet of bases — three-tiered cheesecake anyone...

Definitely been watching too much Bake Off. Now, make sure you can do these questions before you move on.

Q1   Explain how a gene can code for a particular protein.   [2 marks]

Q2   A section of DNA contains the following base sequence: CGATTCGATCCGAATCGATAG How many codons does the section of DNA contain?   [1 mark]

More on Protein Synthesis

This page is all about how you actually use the DNA code to make the proteins that you need.

Proteins are Made in Two Stages

1) Transcription

1) Proteins are made in the cell cytoplasm by subcellular structures called ribosomes (see p.2). DNA is found in the cell nucleus and can't move out of it because it's really big. The cell needs to get the information from the DNA to the ribosome in the cytoplasm.

2) This is done using a molecule called messenger RNA (mRNA). Like DNA, mRNA is made up of a sequence of bases, but it's shorter and only a single strand. It also uses uracil (U) instead of thymine (T) as a base.

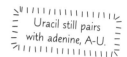
Uracil still pairs with adenine, A-U.

3) RNA polymerase is the enzyme involved in joining together the base sequence to make mRNA. This stage of protein synthesis is called transcription. Here's how it works:

1) RNA polymerase binds to a region of non-coding DNA in front of a gene.

2) The two DNA strands unzip and the RNA polymerase moves along one of the strands of the DNA.

3) It uses the coding DNA in the gene as a template to make the mRNA. Base pairing between the DNA and RNA ensures that the mRNA is complementary to the gene.

4) Once made, the mRNA molecule moves out of the nucleus and joins with a ribosome in the cytoplasm.

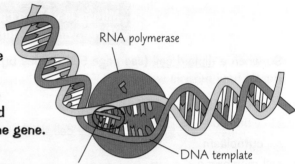

RNA polymerase

DNA template

mRNA molecule forming

2) Translation

Once the mRNA is bound to a ribosome, the protein can be assembled. This stage is called translation.

1) Amino acids are brought to the ribosome by another RNA molecule called transfer RNA (tRNA).

2) The order in which the amino acids are brought to the ribosome matches the order of the codons in mRNA.

3) Part of the tRNA's structure is called an anticodon — it is complementary to the codon for the amino acid. The pairing of the codon and anticodon makes sure that the amino acids are brought to the ribosome in the correct order.

4) The amino acids are joined together by the ribosome. This makes a protein.

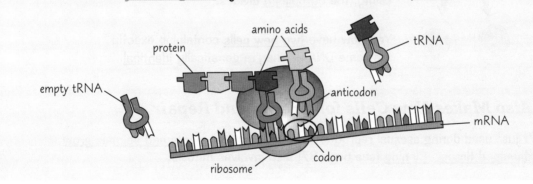

amino acids

protein

tRNA

empty tRNA

anticodon

mRNA

ribosome

codon

Alors, j'adore l'ADN, et les protéines sont aussi bien...

Get it? You have to translate it... Never mind. Remember — the non-coding DNA is in on the action here too.

Q1 Describe how a gene is transcribed to form mRNA. [3 marks]

Paper 2

Asexual Reproduction and Mitosis

There are <u>two ways</u> an organism can <u>reproduce</u> (asexually and sexually) and two ways a cell can <u>divide</u> (mitosis and meiosis). This page, as you might have guessed, is about <u>asexual reproduction</u> and <u>mitosis</u>.

Asexual Reproduction Involves Mitosis

1) An <u>ordinary cell</u> can make a new cell by simply <u>dividing in two</u>. <u>Both new cells</u> are <u>genetically identical</u> to the original cell — they both contain <u>exactly the same</u> genetic information.

2) This type of cell division is known as <u>mitosis</u> (see below).

3) Some organisms <u>produce offspring</u> (children) <u>using mitosis</u>. This is known as <u>asexual reproduction</u>. Organisms which reproduce asexually include <u>bacteria</u> and some <u>plants</u> (see page 61).

> <u>Asexual reproduction</u> involves only <u>one</u> parent. The offspring have <u>identical genes</u> to the parent — so there's <u>no variation</u> between parent and offspring.

Mitosis Produces Genetically Identical Cells

> <u>Mitosis</u> is when a cell reproduces itself by <u>splitting</u> to form <u>two cells</u> with <u>identical sets of chromosomes.</u>

So when a <u>diploid cell</u> (see page 53) divides by mitosis, you get <u>two cells</u> that are <u>both diploid</u>. Here's how mitosis works:

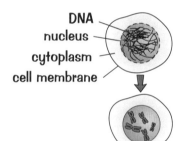

DNA
nucleus
cytoplasm
cell membrane

In a cell that's not dividing, the DNA is all spread out in <u>long strings</u>.

If the cell gets a signal to <u>divide</u>, it needs to <u>duplicate</u> its DNA — so there's one copy for each new cell. The DNA forms <u>X-shaped</u> chromosomes. Each 'arm' of the chromosome is an <u>exact duplicate</u> of the other.

The <u>left arm</u> has the same DNA as the <u>right arm</u> of the chromosome.

The chromosomes then <u>line up</u> at the centre of the cell and <u>cell fibres</u> pull them apart. The <u>two arms</u> of each chromosome go to <u>opposite ends</u> of the cell.

<u>Membranes</u> form around each of the sets of chromosomes. These become the <u>nuclei</u> of the two new cells.

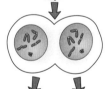

Lastly, the <u>cytoplasm</u> divides.

You now have <u>two new cells</u> containing exactly the same DNA — they're genetically <u>identical</u>.

Mitosis Also Makes New Cells for Growth and Repair

Mitosis isn't just used during asexual reproduction — it's how <u>all plants and animals grow</u> and <u>repair damaged tissue</u>. <u>Cloning</u> (see page 87) also involves mitosis.

A cell's favourite computer game — Divide and Conquer...

So, asexual reproduction takes place using mitosis. There's only one parent involved and the offspring are genetically identical to the parent. Lovely. Now for some variation — time for a bit of sexual reproduction...

Q1   Describe what happens to a cell after it receives a signal to divide by mitosis.   [5 marks]

Sexual Reproduction and Meiosis

Another page, another form of reproduction... Oh, and another type of cell division too. You lucky thing.

Sexual Reproduction Produces Genetically Different Cells

1) Sexual reproduction is where genetic information from two organisms (a father and a mother) is combined to produce offspring which are genetically different to either parent.

2) In sexual reproduction, the mother and father produce gametes. Gametes are sperm cells and egg cells.

3) Gametes are haploid — this means they have half the number of chromosomes in a normal cell. In humans, each gamete contains 23 chromosomes — so the haploid number is 23.

4) At fertilisation, a male gamete fuses with a female gamete to form a zygote (fertilised egg). The zygote ends up with the full set of chromosomes.

5) The zygote then undergoes cell division (by mitosis — see previous page) and develops into an embryo.

6) The embryo inherits features from both parents — it's received a mixture of chromosomes from its mum and its dad (and it's the chromosomes that decide how you turn out).

7) The fertilisation of gametes is random — this produces genetic variation in the offspring.

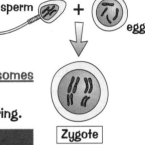

> **Sexual reproduction** involves the **fusion** of **male and female gametes.**
> Because there are **two** parents, the offspring contain a **mixture** of their **parents' genes.**

Gametes are Produced by Meiosis

Meiosis is another type of cell division. It's different to mitosis (on the previous page) because it doesn't produce identical cells. In humans, meiosis only happens in the reproductive organs (ovaries and testes).

> Meiosis produces four haploid cells whose chromosomes are not identical.

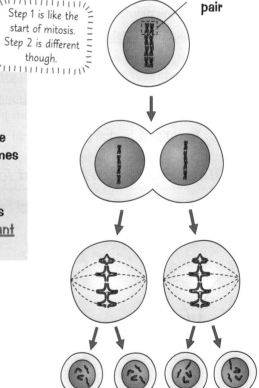

chromosome pair

Division 1

1) Before the cell starts to divide, it duplicates its DNA (so there's enough for each new cell). One arm of each X-shaped chromosome is an exact copy of the other arm.

Step 1 is like the start of mitosis. Step 2 is different though.

2) In the first division in meiosis (there are two divisions) the chromosomes line up in pairs in the centre of the cell. One chromosome in each pair came from the organism's mother and one came from its father.

3) The pairs are then pulled apart, so each new cell only has one copy of each chromosome. Some of the father's chromosomes (shown in red) and some of the mother's chromosomes (shown in blue) go into each new cell.

4) Each new cell will have a mixture of the mother's and father's chromosomes. Mixing up the genes like this is really important — it creates genetic variation in the offspring.

Division 2

5) In the second division the chromosomes line up again in the centre of the cell. It's a lot like mitosis. The arms of the chromosomes are pulled apart.

6) You get four haploid gametes. Each gamete only has a single set of chromosomes. The gametes are all genetically different.

Now that I have your undivided attention...

Remember — in humans, meiosis only occurs in the reproductive organs, where gametes are made.

Q1   How does meiosis introduce genetic variation?   [2 marks]

Sexual Reproduction in Plants

Some types of plants reproduce <u>asexually</u> (see page 61), whilst others reproduce <u>sexually</u> (see below).

The Flower Contains both Male and Female Gametes

Flowering plants have both <u>male</u> and <u>female structures</u> — they're contained in the <u>flower</u>:

The Stamen is the Male Reproductive Part

The <u>stamen</u> consists of the <u>anther</u> and <u>filament</u>:

- The <u>anther</u> contains <u>pollen grains</u> — these produce the <u>male gametes</u> (sperm).
- The <u>filament</u> is the <u>stalk</u> that <u>supports</u> the anther.

The Carpel is the Female Reproductive Part

The <u>carpel</u> consists of the <u>ovary</u>, <u>style</u> and <u>stigma</u>.

- The <u>stigma</u> is the <u>end</u> bit that the <u>pollen</u> grains <u>attach</u> to.
- The <u>style</u> is the rod-like section that <u>supports</u> the stigma.
- The <u>ovary</u> contains the <u>female gametes</u> (eggs) inside <u>ovules</u>.

1) <u>Pollination</u> is the <u>transfer of pollen</u> from an <u>anther</u> to a <u>stigma</u>, so that the male gametes can <u>fertilise</u> the female gametes in sexual reproduction.
2) <u>Cross-pollination</u> is a type of <u>sexual reproduction</u> where pollen is transferred from the anther of <u>one plant</u> to the stigma of <u>another</u>.
3) Plants that cross-pollinate <u>rely</u> on things like <u>insects</u> or the <u>wind</u> to help them pollinate.

Some Plants are Adapted for Insect Pollination

Here's how plants can be <u>adapted</u> for <u>pollination by insects</u>...

1) They have <u>brightly coloured petals</u> to <u>attract insects</u>.
2) They also have <u>scented flowers</u> and <u>nectaries</u> (glands that secrete <u>nectar</u>) to <u>attract insects</u>.
3) They make <u>big, sticky pollen grains</u> — the grains <u>stick to insects</u> as they go from plant to plant.
4) The <u>stigma</u> is also <u>sticky</u> so that any <u>pollen</u> picked up by insects on other plants will <u>stick to the stigma</u>.

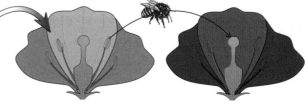

Other Plants are Adapted for Wind Pollination

Features of plants that are <u>adapted</u> for <u>pollination by wind</u> include...

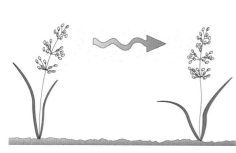

1) <u>Small</u>, <u>dull petals</u> on the flower (they don't need to attract insects).
2) <u>No nectaries</u> or strong <u>scents</u> (for the same reason).
3) A <u>lot</u> of <u>pollen</u> grains — they're <u>small</u> and <u>light</u> so that they can easily be <u>carried</u> by the wind.
4) <u>Long filaments</u> that <u>hang</u> the anthers <u>outside</u> the flower, so that a lot of the <u>pollen</u> gets <u>blown away</u> by the wind.
5) A <u>large</u> and <u>feathery stigma</u> to <u>catch pollen</u> as it's carried past by the wind. The stigma often <u>hangs outside</u> the flower too.

There are no "B"s in wind pollination — bzzzz bzzz bzzzz...

It's a bit weird to think of plants reproducing sexually — it just means that the male gametes (in the pollen) fertilise the female gametes (in the ovary). Not quite so weird after all.

Q1   Explain two adaptations that a wind-pollinated flower has for pollination.   [4 marks]

Fertilisation and Germination in Plants

Once the pollen has found its way to a lovely stigma, it's time for fertilisation to take place...

Fertilisation is the Fusion of Gametes

1) A pollen grain lands on the stigma of a flower, usually with help from insects or the wind (see previous page).

2) A pollen tube grows out of the pollen grain and down through the style to the ovary and into the ovule.

3) A nucleus from the male gamete moves down the tube to join with a female gamete in the ovule. Fertilisation is when the two nuclei fuse together to make a zygote. This divides by mitosis to form an embryo.

4) Each fertilised female gamete forms a seed. The ovary develops into a fruit around the seed.

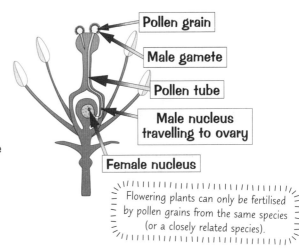

Flowering plants can only be fertilised by pollen grains from the same species (or a closely related species).

Germination is when Seeds Start to Grow

A seed will often lie dormant until the conditions around it are right for germination. Seeds need the right conditions to start germinating:

1) Water — to activate the enzymes that break down the food reserves in the seed.

2) Oxygen — for respiration (see page 29), which transfers the energy from food for growth.

3) A suitable temperature — for the enzymes inside the seed to work. This depends on what type of seed it is.

first green leaves

Germination only starts when all these conditions are suitable.

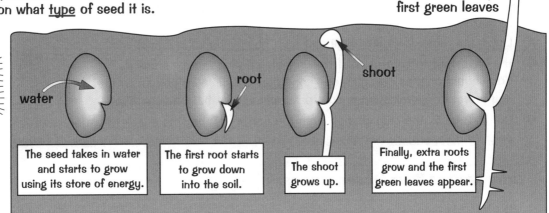

water

root

shoot

The seed takes in water and starts to grow using its store of energy.

The first root starts to grow down into the soil.

The shoot grows up.

Finally, extra roots grow and the first green leaves appear.

Germinating Seeds get Energy from Food Stores

1) A developed seed contains an embryo and a store of food reserves, wrapped in a hard seed coat.

2) When a seed starts to germinate, it gets glucose for respiration from its own food store. This transfers the energy it needs to grow.

3) Once the plant has grown enough to produce green leaves (see above), it can get its own food for energy from photosynthesis (see page 20).

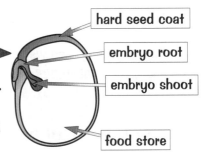

hard seed coat

embryo root

embryo shoot

food store

I went out for dinner with my German friend — he germinated...

Phew, what a palaver. It all starts with flowers, which lead to pollination, then fertilisation and onto seed development. Finally they germinate and blossom into fully-fledged plants surviving on their own far away from their parents.

Q1 Describe how germinating seeds get the energy needed for growth. [2 marks]

PRACTICAL Investigating Seed Germination

If you've always wanted to investigate the different conditions needed for germination to take place, then today is your lucky day...

You Can Investigate the Conditions Needed for Germination

You saw on the last page that seeds need water, oxygen and a suitable temperature for germination to happen. Here's an experiment you can do to investigate these conditions.

1) Take four boiling tubes and put some cotton wool at the bottom of each one.

2) Put 10 seeds on top of the cotton wool in each boiling tube.

3) Set up each boiling tube as follows:

> Tube 1   water, oxygen, room temperature (the control).
> Tube 2   no water, oxygen, room temperature.
> Tube 3   water, oxygen, low temperature.
> Tube 4   water, no oxygen, room temperature.

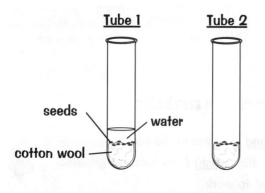

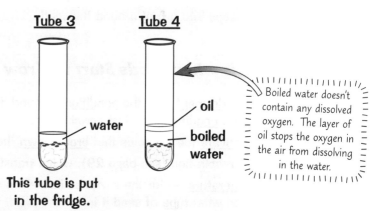

Boiled water doesn't contain any dissolved oxygen. The layer of oil stops the oxygen in the air from dissolving in the water.

This tube is put in the fridge.

4) Leave the tubes for a few days and then observe what has happened.

5) It's important to control all of the variables during the experiment. You should only be changing one condition at a time so you know that any effect on germination is due to the change in that one condition.

6) So, in Tube 2, the only change from the control (Tube 1) is a lack of water. In Tube 3, only the temperature has changed. In Tube 4, the only change is the lack of oxygen.

Interpreting Your Observations   new, internal

1) You should only see germination happening in Tube 1.

2) This is because all of the conditions needed for germination are present.

3) The seeds in the other boiling tubes won't germinate — this shows that the seeds need water, oxygen and a suitable temperature to germinate.

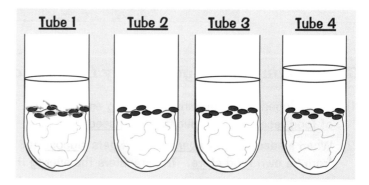

How do you stop an angry seed from germinating? Get it to chill out...

Seeds need to have water, oxygen and a suitable temperature to germinate. So even if you have the perfect amount of water and oxygen, if the temperature isn't right, your seeds are just going to sit there doing nothing. Lazy.

Q1   A student is investigating germination. She puts some moist cotton wool in a boiling tube.
She then puts ten seeds on top of the cotton wool and puts the boiling tube in the fridge.
After five days, she looks at the seeds in the boiling tube.
a) Describe what observation you would expect the student to make.   [1 mark]
b) Explain the reason for this observation.   [1 mark]

Section 7 — Reproduction and Inheritance

Asexual Reproduction in Plants

Some plants reproduce <u>asexually</u>. They do this in the wild (<u>naturally</u>) and when we force them to (<u>artificially</u>). Artificial asexual reproduction is also called <u>cloning</u>.

Plants Can Reproduce Asexually Using Natural Methods...

Plants have several different ways of reproducing asexually.
Some plants do so by growing <u>new plants</u> from their stems — for example, <u>strawberry plants</u>...

1) The parent strawberry plant sends out <u>runners</u> — <u>fast-growing stems</u> that grow out <u>sideways</u>, just above the ground.

2) The runners <u>take root</u> at various points (a short distance away) and <u>new plants</u> start to grow.

3) The new plants are <u>clones</u> of the <u>parent</u> strawberry plant, so there's <u>no</u> genetic variation between them.

> Some plants reproduce asexually <u>and</u> sexually, e.g. strawberry plants send out runners and produce fruit (seeds).

runner

parent plant

new plant

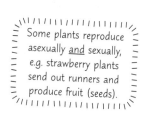

...or We Can Clone Them Using Artificial Methods

Asexual reproduction can be used to <u>clone plants</u>. And it's not all high-tech crazy science stuff either — gardeners have been using <u>cuttings</u> since before your gran was knee-high to a grasshopper.

1) Gardeners can take <u>cuttings</u> from good parent plants, and then plant them to produce <u>genetically identical copies</u> (clones) of the parent plant.

2) These plants can be produced <u>quickly and cheaply</u>.

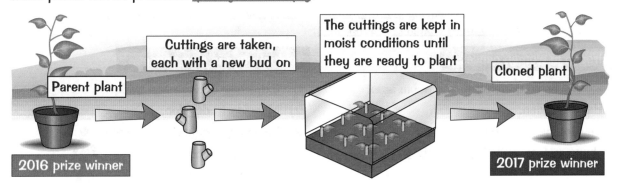

Parent plant

2016 prize winner

Cuttings are taken, each with a new bud on

The cuttings are kept in moist conditions until they are ready to plant

Cloned plant

2017 prize winner

You may need to reproduce these facts in the exam...

Cloning plants is great because you can produce loads of plants with the same great characteristics. But this also comes at a price — if a disease hits or the environment changes, the whole population could be badly affected.

Q1   Suggest one advantage of growing plants from cuttings.   [1 mark]

Human Reproductive Systems

If you skipped to this page in the book first, shame on you... But now you're here, it's time to learn all about the <u>male</u> and <u>female reproductive systems</u> — with a little bit on <u>sex hormones</u> thrown in for good measure.

The Male Reproductive System Makes Sperm

1) Sperm are <u>male gametes</u>. They're made in the <u>testes</u>, <u>all the time</u> after puberty.

2) Sperm mix with a <u>liquid</u> to make <u>semen</u>, which is <u>ejaculated</u> from the penis into the <u>vagina</u> of the female during <u>sexual intercourse</u>.

See page 57 for more on gametes.

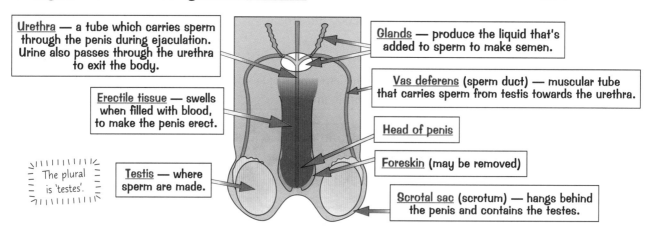

<u>Urethra</u> — a tube which carries sperm through the penis during ejaculation. Urine also passes through the urethra to exit the body.

<u>Erectile tissue</u> — swells when filled with blood, to make the penis erect.

The plural is 'testes'.

<u>Testis</u> — where sperm are made.

<u>Glands</u> — produce the liquid that's added to sperm to make semen.

<u>Vas deferens</u> (sperm duct) — muscular tube that carries sperm from testis towards the urethra.

<u>Head of penis</u>

<u>Foreskin</u> (may be removed)

<u>Scrotal sac</u> (scrotum) — hangs behind the penis and contains the testes.

The Female Reproductive System Makes Ova (Eggs)

1) Ova are <u>female gametes</u>. An <u>ovum</u> (egg) is produced <u>every 28 days</u> from one of the two <u>ovaries</u>.

2) It then passes into the <u>Fallopian tube</u> — this is where it might <u>meet sperm</u> that have entered the vagina during <u>sexual intercourse</u>.

3) If it <u>isn't fertilised</u> by sperm, the ovum will <u>break up</u> and pass out of the <u>vagina</u>.

4) If it <u>is fertilised</u>, the ovum starts to divide. The new cells will travel down the Fallopian tube to the <u>uterus</u> (womb) and attach to the <u>endometrium</u> (uterus lining). A fertilised ovum develops into an <u>embryo</u>.

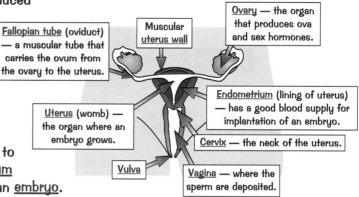

<u>Fallopian tube</u> (oviduct) — a muscular tube that carries the ovum from the ovary to the uterus.

<u>Muscular uterus wall</u>

<u>Ovary</u> — the organ that produces ova and sex hormones.

<u>Endometrium</u> (lining of uterus) — has a good blood supply for implantation of an embryo.

<u>Uterus</u> (womb) — the organ where an embryo grows.

<u>Cervix</u> — the neck of the uterus.

<u>Vulva</u>

<u>Vagina</u> — where the sperm are deposited.

Hormones Promote Sexual Characteristics at Puberty

At puberty, your body starts releasing <u>sex hormones</u> — <u>testosterone</u> in men and <u>oestrogen</u> in women. These trigger off the <u>secondary sexual characteristics</u>:

Oestrogen in women causes...

1) <u>Extra hair</u> on underarms and pubic area.
2) <u>Hips</u> to <u>widen</u>.
3) Development of <u>breasts</u>.
4) <u>Ovum</u> release and <u>start of periods</u>.

Testosterone in men causes...

1) <u>Extra hair</u> on face and body.
2) <u>Muscles</u> to <u>develop</u>.
3) <u>Penis and testicles</u> to enlarge.
4) <u>Sperm</u> production.
5) <u>Deepening</u> of <u>voice</u>.

See page 48 for more on hormones.

Phew — who'd be a teenager...

I have my suspicions that you won't have too much difficulty remembering most of this stuff.
Nevertheless, make sure you learn everything on this page, so you don't throw away easy marks in the exam.

Q1   Give three secondary sexual characteristics that develop in response to the release of oestrogen.   [3 marks]

The Menstrual Cycle and Pregnancy

Starting in puberty, females undergo a monthly sequence of events — the menstrual cycle.
This involves the body preparing the uterus (womb) in case it receives a fertilised ovum (egg).

The Menstrual Cycle Has Four Stages

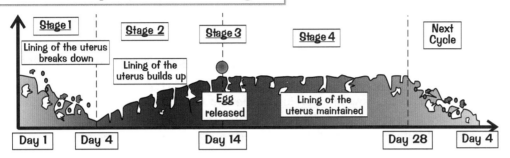

Stage 1 Day 1 — menstruation starts. The uterus lining breaks down for about four days.

Stage 2 The uterus lining builds up again, from day 4 to day 14, into a thick
spongy layer full of blood vessels, ready to receive a fertilised egg.

Stage 3 An egg develops and is released from the ovary at day 14 — this is called ovulation.

Stage 4 The wall is then maintained for about 14 days until day 28. If no fertilised egg has landed on the
uterus wall by day 28, the spongy lining starts to break down and the whole cycle starts again.

It's Controlled by Four Hormones

Paper 2

1 FSH (Follicle-Stimulating Hormone)
1) Produced in the pituitary gland.
2) Causes an egg to mature in one of the ovaries,
   in a structure called a follicle.
3) Stimulates the ovaries to produce oestrogen.
4) Oestrogen then inhibits the release of FSH.

Paper 2

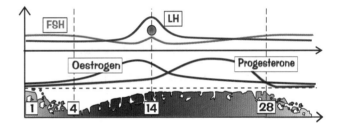

2 Oestrogen
1) Produced in the ovaries.
2) Causes the lining of the uterus to grow.
3) Stimulates the release of LH
   (which causes the release of an egg).

Paper 2

3 LH (Luteinising Hormone)
1) Produced by the pituitary gland.
2) Stimulates the release of an egg at day 14 (ovulation).

Paper 2

4 Progesterone
1) Produced in the ovaries by the remains of
   the follicle after ovulation.
2) Maintains the lining of the uterus during the
   second half of the cycle. When the level of
   progesterone falls, the lining breaks down.
3) Inhibits the release of LH and FSH.

The Embryo Develops During Pregnancy

Once an ovum has been fertilised, it develops into an embryo and implants in the uterus.
In later stages of pregnancy (when it starts to look human) the embryo is called a fetus.

Once the embryo has implanted,
the placenta develops — this lets
the blood of the embryo and mother
get very close to allow the exchange
of food, oxygen and waste.

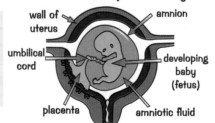

The amnion membrane forms —
this surrounds the embryo and is
full of amniotic fluid. Amniotic
fluid protects the embryo against
knocks and bumps.

Female or not — you've still got to know all this...

In the exam, you might get graphs like the ones above and be asked to explain which hormone causes what.

Q1   Describe the role of the placenta during pregnancy.   [1 mark]

64

Genetic Diagrams

This page is all about how <u>characteristics</u> (like eye colour) are <u>inherited</u>. Before you start, you might want to refresh your memory of <u>genes</u>, <u>chromosomes</u> and <u>DNA</u> on page 53. It'll make life a lot easier, trust me.

Alleles are Different Versions of the Same Gene

1) What <u>genes</u> you <u>inherit</u> control what <u>characteristics</u> you <u>develop</u>. Some characteristics are controlled by a <u>single gene</u>. However <u>most</u> characteristics are controlled by <u>several genes interacting</u>.

2) Most of the time you have <u>two copies</u> of each gene (i.e. <u>two alleles</u>, see p.53) — one from each parent.

3) If the alleles are different, you have <u>instructions</u> for <u>two different versions</u> of a characteristic (e.g. blue eyes or brown eyes) but you only <u>show one version</u> of the two (e.g. brown eyes). The version of the characteristic that appears is caused by the <u>dominant allele</u>. The other allele is said to be <u>recessive</u>. The characteristic caused by the recessive allele only appears if <u>both alleles</u> are recessive.

4) Your <u>genotype</u> is the <u>alleles</u> that you have. Your <u>phenotype</u> is the <u>characteristics</u> the alleles produce.

5) In genetic diagrams, <u>letters</u> are used to represent <u>genes</u>. <u>Dominant alleles</u> are always shown with a <u>capital letter</u> (e.g. 'C') and <u>recessive alleles</u> with a <u>small letter</u> (e.g. 'c').

6) If you're <u>homozygous</u> for a trait you have <u>two alleles the same</u> for that particular gene, e.g. CC or cc. If you're <u>heterozygous</u> for a trait you have <u>two different alleles</u> for that particular gene, e.g. Cc.

7) Some characteristics are caused by <u>codominant alleles</u>. Neither allele is recessive, so you <u>show characteristics</u> from <u>both alleles</u> (e.g. not blood group A or B, but blood group <u>AB</u>).

Genetic Diagrams show the Possible Alleles in the Offspring

The inheritance of a <u>single</u> characteristic is called <u>monohybrid inheritance</u>. You can use a <u>monohybrid cross</u> to show how <u>recessive</u> and <u>dominant</u> traits for a <u>single characteristic</u> are inherited.

When you breed two organisms together to look at one trait, it's called a monohybrid cross.

Imagine you're cross-breeding <u>hamsters</u>, and that some have <u>superpowers</u>. And suppose you know that the behaviour is due to <u>one gene</u>...

Let's say that the allele which causes the superpowers is <u>recessive</u> — so use a '<u>b</u>'. And normal behaviour is due to a <u>dominant allele</u> — call it '<u>B</u>'.

1) A <u>superpowered</u> hamster <u>must</u> have the <u>genotype bb</u> (i.e. it must be homozygous for this trait).

2) However, a <u>normal hamster</u> could have <u>two</u> possible genotypes — BB (homozygous) or Bb (heterozygous), because the dominant allele (B) <u>overrules</u> the recessive one (b).

3) Here's what happens if you breed from two <u>heterozygous</u> hamsters:

There's a <u>75% chance</u> of having a normal hamster, and a <u>25% chance</u> of a superpowered one. To put that another way... you'd expect a <u>3 : 1 ratio</u> of normal : superpowered hamsters. This ratio is called a <u>phenotypic ratio</u> (because it's a ratio of different phenotypes).

The lines show all the possible ways the parents' alleles could combine. Remember, only one of these possibilities would actually happen for any one offspring.

4) If you breed <u>two homozygous</u> hamsters there's only <u>one possible offspring</u> you can end up with. For example, breeding BB and bb hamsters can only give offspring with a Bb genotype — and they'd all have a normal phenotype.

What do you get if you cross a kangaroo and a sheep...

...a ratio of 1 : 1 kangsheep to sheeparoos... bet you thought I was going to say a woolly jumper. At first glance this stuff can look quite confusing, but the more you go over it, the more it makes sense.

Q1 Define genotype and phenotype. [2 marks]

Section 7 — Reproduction and Inheritance

More Genetic Diagrams

Just when you thought it was safe to turn over... <u>More genetic diagrams</u>. Mwa ha haaa. Ahem.
Actually they're really not that bad. And I've given you lots of <u>lovely examples</u> to help you out.

There's Another Way to Draw Genetic Diagrams

You can also draw a type of genetic diagram called a <u>Punnett square</u>.
They're dead easy to do. You start by drawing a <u>grid</u> like this.

Then you <u>fill it in</u> like this:

1) Put the <u>possible gametes</u> from <u>one</u> parent down the side,
    and those from the <u>other</u> parent along the top.

2) In each middle square, <u>fill in</u> the letters from the top and side that <u>line up</u> with that square.
    The <u>pairs of letters</u> in the middle show the possible combinations of the gametes.

For example:

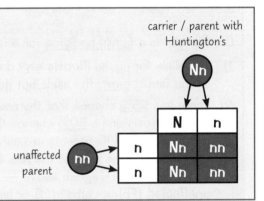

1) <u>Huntington's</u> is a genetic disorder of the <u>nervous system</u>.
2) The disorder is caused by a <u>dominant allele</u>, 'N', and so can
    be inherited if just <u>one parent</u> carries the defective gene.
3) The parent who carries the gene will also have the disorder
    since the allele is dominant, but the <u>symptoms</u> don't start
    to appear until <u>after</u> the person is about 40.
4) As the Punnett square shows, a person carrying the N allele
    has a <u>50% chance</u> of passing it on to each of their children.
5) There's also a <u>1 : 1 phenotypic ratio</u> in the children of
    carrier : unaffected child.

You Can Draw Genetic Diagrams for Codominant Inheritance too

You might need to work out the outcome of a monohybrid cross
involving <u>codominant alleles</u> (see previous page).

Don't worry, it's pretty straightforward — you can use a <u>genetic diagram</u> like the ones above to help you.

Here's an example:

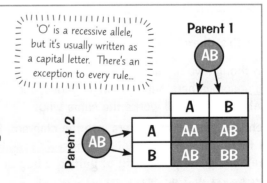

'O' is a recessive allele, but it's usually written as a capital letter. There's an exception to every rule...

1) Your <u>blood type</u> is determined by <u>two codominant</u>
    <u>alleles</u> (<u>A</u> and <u>B</u>) and one recessive one (O).

2) Blood can be <u>type A</u> (AA or AO genotype),
    <u>type B</u> (BB or BO genotype), <u>type AB</u>
    (AB genotype) or <u>type O</u> (OO genotype).

3) As the Punnett square shows, for two people with
    <u>type AB</u> blood there's a <u>50% chance</u> their children
    will be type AB, a <u>25% chance</u> they'll be type A
    and a <u>25% chance</u> they'll be type B.

Paper 2

Personally, I prefer strawberries in my Punnett squares...

They might ask you to draw a genetic diagram in the exam. It's nothing to panic about though — they all work the
same way. So go over all the examples on this page (and the previous one) until you're happy with them.

Q1   In merpeople, the dominant allele, T, causes a long tail and the recessive allele, t, causes a short tail.
     Using a Punnett square, predict the ratio of long to short tailed merbabies for a cross between
     a heterozygous merman and a mermaid who is homozygous recessive for tail length.   [3 marks]

Family Pedigrees and Sex Determination

Bit of a mixed bag this page — still, it makes life just a tad more exciting...

You Need to Understand Family Pedigrees

Knowing how inheritance works helps you to interpret a family pedigree (a family tree of genetic disorders). Here's a worked example using cystic fibrosis — a genetic disorder of the cell membranes.

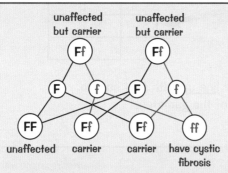

unaffected but carrier — Ff
unaffected but carrier — Ff

F f F f

FF — unaffected
Ff — carrier
Ff — carrier
ff — have cystic fibrosis

1) The allele which causes cystic fibrosis is a recessive allele, 'f', carried by about 1 person in 30.

2) Because it's recessive, people with only one copy of the allele won't have the disorder — they're known as carriers.

3) For a child to have a chance of inheriting the disorder, both parents must either have the disorder themselves or be carriers.

4) As the diagram shows, there's a 1 in 4 chance of a child having the disorder if both parents are carriers.

On the right is a family pedigree for a family that includes carriers of cystic fibrosis.

1) The allele for cystic fibrosis isn't dominant because plenty of the family carry the allele but don't have the disorder.

2) There is a 25% chance that the new baby will have cystic fibrosis and a 50% chance that it will be a carrier because both of its parents are carriers but do not have the disorder. The case of the new baby is just the same as in the genetic diagram above — so the baby could be unaffected (FF), a carrier (Ff) or have cystic fibrosis (ff).

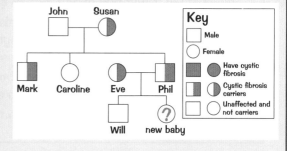

John   Susan

Mark   Caroline   Eve   Phil

Will   new baby

Key
- Male
- Female
- Have cystic fibrosis
- Cystic fibrosis carriers
- Unaffected and not carriers

Your Chromosomes Control Whether You're Male or Female

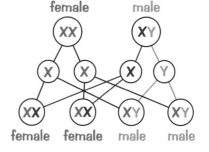

Congratulations! It's an XX.

There are 23 matched pairs of chromosomes in every human body cell. The 23rd pair is labelled XX or XY. They're the two chromosomes that decide whether you turn out male or female.

- Males have an X and a Y chromosome: XY
  The Y chromosome causes male characteristics.

- Females have two X chromosomes: XX
  The XX combination causes female characteristics.

This is true for all mammals, but not for some other organisms, e.g. plants.

Because of this, there's an equal chance of having either a boy or a girl. Here's a genetic diagram to prove it.

1) Even though we're talking about inheriting chromosomes here and not single genes, the genetic diagram still works the same way.

2) When you plug all the letters into the diagram, it shows that there are two XX results and two XY results, so there's the same probability of getting a boy or a girl.

3) Don't forget that this 50 : 50 ratio is only a probability. If you had four kids they could all be boys.

female   male
XX   XY

X X X Y

XX   XX   XY   XY
female female male male

All eggs have one X chromosome, but a sperm can have either an X chromosome or a Y chromosome. So sex determination in humans depends on whether the sperm that fertilises an egg carries an X or a Y.

Have you got the Y-factor...

I bet you're sick of genetic diagrams by now. Still, that family pedigree makes a nice change. Umm... sort of.

Q1 Use the family pedigree above for the following question. Mark and his wife (who is not shown in the diagram) have a baby with cystic fibrosis. What are the possible genotypes of Mark's wife? [1 mark]

Variation

The word '<u>variation</u>' sounds pretty fancy. All it means is how animals or plants of the same species <u>look or behave slightly differently from each other</u>. There are two kinds of variation — <u>genetic</u> and <u>environmental</u>.

Genetic Variation is Caused by... Genes (Surprise)

1) All <u>animals</u> (including humans) are bound to be <u>slightly different</u> from each other because their <u>genes</u> are slightly different.

2) You might remember from p.53 that genes determine how your body turns out — they control your <u>inherited traits</u>, e.g. <u>eye colour</u>. We all end up with a <u>different</u> set of genes. The <u>exceptions</u> to this rule are <u>identical twins</u>, because their genes are <u>exactly the same</u>.

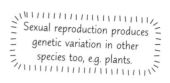
Sexual reproduction produces genetic variation in other species too, e.g. plants.

Most Variation in Animals is Due to Genes AND Environment

1) Most variation in animals is caused by a <u>mixture</u> of genetic and environmental factors.

2) Almost every single aspect of a human (or other animal) is <u>affected by our environment</u> in some way, however small. In fact it's a lot <u>easier</u> to list the factors which <u>aren't</u> affected in any way by environment:

- <u>Eye colour</u>,
- <u>Hair colour</u> in most animals (in humans, vanity plays a big part),
- <u>Inherited disorders</u> like haemophilia, cystic fibrosis, etc.,
- <u>Blood group</u>.

3) <u>Environment</u> can have a large effect on human growth even <u>before</u> someone's born. For example, a baby's <u>weight</u> at birth can be affected by the mother's <u>diet</u>.

4) And having a <u>poor diet</u> whilst you're growing up can <u>stunt your growth</u> — another environmental variation.

5) For some characteristics, it's <u>hard to say</u> which factor is more important — genes or environment...

- <u>Health</u> — Some people are more likely to get certain <u>diseases</u> (e.g. <u>cancer</u> and <u>heart disease</u>) because of their genes. But <u>lifestyle</u> also affects the risk, e.g. if you smoke or only eat junk food.
- <u>Intelligence</u> — One theory is that although your <u>maximum possible IQ</u> might be determined by your <u>genes</u>, whether you get to it depends on your <u>environment</u>, e.g. your <u>upbringing</u> and <u>school</u> life.
- <u>Sporting ability</u> — Again, genes probably determine your <u>potential</u>, but training is important too.

Environmental Variation in Plants is Much Greater

Plants are strongly affected by:

1) <u>sunlight</u>,   2) <u>moisture level</u>,   3) <u>temperature</u>,   4) the <u>mineral content</u> of the <u>soil</u>.

For example, plants may grow <u>twice as big</u> or <u>twice as fast</u> due to <u>fairly modest</u> changes in environment such as the amount of <u>sunlight</u> or <u>rainfall</u> they're getting, or how <u>warm</u> it is or what the <u>soil</u> is like.

Environmental variation — like sun and scattered showers...

So, all the variation that you see around you is a complicated mixture of environmental and genetic influences. In fact, it's often really tricky to decide which factor is more influential, your genes or the environment.

Q1   Give two environmental factors which lead to variation in plants.   [2 marks]

Evolution and Natural Selection

The <u>theory of evolution</u> states that one of your (probably very distant) ancestors was a <u>blob</u> in a swamp somewhere. Something like that, anyway. It's probably best to read on for more details...

Make Sure You Know the Theory of Evolution

Theory of evolution: Life began as simple organisms from which more complex organisms evolved (rather than just popping into existence).

The whole <u>process</u> of evolution usually takes place gradually over <u>millions of years</u>. It's still going on today, e.g. some <u>bacteria</u> are evolving to become <u>resistant to antibiotics</u> (see the next page).

Natural Selection Means the "Survival of the Fittest"

<u>Charles Darwin</u> came up with the theory of <u>evolution by natural selection</u>. At the time, he didn't know how <u>characteristics</u> were passed on to <u>offspring</u> — but we now know that they're passed on in the <u>genes</u> that parents contribute to their offspring. Scientists have developed Darwin's theory over time, using what we now know about genetics.

Charles Darwin

1) Darwin knew that organisms in a species show <u>variation</u> in their characteristics.
2) Darwin also knew that the <u>resources</u> that organisms need to survive are <u>limited</u> and individuals have to <u>compete</u> for these resources to <u>survive</u>.
3) Darwin concluded that the organisms with the <u>most suitable characteristics</u> for the environment would be <u>more successful competitors</u> and so would have a <u>better chance</u> of survival — this is known as the "<u>survival of the fittest</u>".
4) The successful organisms will then have an increased chance of <u>breeding</u> and passing on their <u>genes</u>.
5) This means that a <u>greater</u> proportion of individuals in the next generation will have the better <u>alleles</u>, and so the <u>characteristics</u>, that help <u>survival</u>.
6) Over many generations, the <u>characteristic</u> that <u>increases survival</u> becomes <u>more common</u> in the population, making the species become better and better able to <u>survive</u>. The 'best' features are <u>naturally selected</u> and the species becomes more and more <u>adapted</u> to its environment. Here's an example:

Once upon a time maybe all rabbits had <u>short ears</u> and managed OK. Then one day out popped a rabbit with <u>big ears</u> who could hear better and was always the first to dive for cover at the sound of a predator. Pretty soon he's fathered a whole family of rabbits with <u>big ears</u>, all diving for cover before the other rabbits, and before you know it there are only <u>big-eared</u> rabbits left — because the rest just didn't hear trouble coming quick enough. FOX!

This is how populations <u>adapt</u> to survive better in their environment (an organism doesn't actually change when it's alive — changes only occur from generation to generation).

The Best Genes for a Particular Environment Tend to Survive

1) The individuals who are <u>less suited</u> to an environment are <u>less likely</u> to survive than those that are better suited, and so have <u>less chance</u> to pass their <u>alleles</u> on. Gradually, over time, this results in a population which is extremely <u>well suited</u> to the environment in which it lives.
2) Remember — <u>variations</u> that are caused by the <u>environment</u> itself (e.g. accidentally losing a finger) <u>aren't</u> involved in natural selection. Variations in a species can have either <u>environmental</u> or <u>genetic causes</u>, but only the <u>genetic</u> ones are passed on to the next generation and influence the <u>evolution</u> of the species.

"Natural Selection" — sounds like vegan chocolates...

So if an organism inherits great genes, it will have a much better shot at surviving. But remember, in terms of evolution, it's no good an organism being great at surviving if it doesn't breed and pass on its genes.

Q1 Musk oxen have thick fur, which is advantageous in the cold climate in which they live. Explain how the musk may have developed this characteristic over many years. [4 marks]

Mutations and Antibiotic Resistance

Everyone is <u>slightly different</u>. One reason for this is that we have different sets of <u>alleles</u>.
This is partly because of how <u>sexual reproduction</u> works (see page 57) and partly due to <u>mutation</u>.

Mutations are Changes to the Genetic Code

1) <u>Occasionally</u> a gene may <u>mutate</u>. A mutation is a <u>rare</u>, <u>random change</u> in an organism's <u>DNA</u> that can be <u>inherited</u>.

2) Mutations <u>change the sequence</u> of the <u>DNA bases</u> in a gene, which produces a <u>genetic variant</u> (a different form of the gene). As the <u>sequence</u> of DNA bases <u>codes</u> for the sequence of <u>amino acids</u> that make up a <u>protein</u> (see page 54), mutations to a gene <u>sometimes</u> lead to <u>changes</u> in the protein that it codes for.

> <u>Enzymes</u> are proteins which need an active site with a <u>very specific shape</u> to be able to work properly. A mutation in the gene that codes for an enzyme could lead to a <u>change in the shape</u> of an enzyme's active site — altering its function. A mutation could also <u>stop the production</u> of the enzyme altogether.

3) Mutations can lead to a different <u>phenotype</u>, <u>increasing variation</u>.

- <u>Most</u> mutations have <u>no effect</u> on the phenotype — they're neutral. For example, if the mutation occurs in an unimportant region of the DNA, or if a mutated codon still codes for the same amino acid, the protein's <u>structure</u> and <u>function</u> will be <u>unaffected</u>. A mutation will also usually have no effect if it occurs in a <u>recessive</u> allele.

  See page 54 for more on codons.

- <u>Some</u> mutations have a <u>small effect</u> on the phenotype. This happens when the change in amino acid only has a <u>slight effect</u> on the protein's structure and function — so the individual's characteristics are only altered <u>very slightly</u>.

- Very <u>rarely</u>, a mutation will have a <u>significant effect</u> on phenotype. For example, it might result in a <u>very different</u> protein which can <u>no longer</u> carry out its function. These mutations can be <u>harmful</u> (such as those which lead to cancer) or <u>beneficial</u> (giving a survival advantage, e.g. antibiotic resistance in bacteria — see below).

4) Mutations can happen <u>spontaneously</u> — when a chromosome doesn't quite copy itself properly. However, the chance of mutation is <u>increased</u> by exposing yourself to:

- <u>ionising radiation</u>, e.g. X-rays, gamma rays or ultraviolet rays,
- <u>chemicals</u> called <u>mutagens</u>, e.g. chemicals in tobacco.

  If the mutations can lead to cancer then the chemicals causing them are called carcinogens.

Bacteria can Evolve and Become Antibiotic-Resistant

1) Like all organisms, bacteria sometimes develop <u>random mutations</u> in their DNA. These can lead to <u>changes</u> in a bacterium's characteristics. Sometimes, they mean that a bacterium is <u>less affected</u> by a particular <u>antibiotic</u>.

2) For the bacterium, this ability to resist antibiotics is a big <u>advantage</u>. It's better able to survive, even in a host who's being treated to get rid of the infection, so it lives for longer and <u>reproduces</u> many more times.

3) This leads to the <u>allele</u> for resistance being <u>passed on</u> to lots of offspring — it's just <u>natural selection</u>. This is how it spreads and becomes <u>more common</u> in a population of bacteria over time.

4) This is a problem for people who become <u>infected</u> with these bacteria, because you <u>can't</u> easily get rid of them with antibiotics. Sometimes drug companies can come up with a <u>new</u> antibiotic that's effective, but '<u>superbugs</u>' that are resistant to most known antibiotics (e.g. MRSA) are becoming more common.

Making sure you finish the whole course of any prescribed antibiotics helps to prevent the spread of antibiotic resistance. Doctors only prescribing antibiotics when they're really needed helps too.

Some mutations make you find revising enjoyable...

Mutations might sound alarming, but actually most are tiny changes that don't affect phenotype at all.

Q1   Explain how antibiotic resistance can increase in a population of bacteria.   [5 marks]

Paper 2

Revision Questions for Section 7

Well, that wraps up Section 7 — yippee. Now here's a thrilling page of questions to test your knowledge.
- Try these questions and tick off each one when you get it right.
- When you've done all the questions for a topic and are completely happy with it, tick off the topic.

DNA and Protein Synthesis (p.53-55) ☐

1) What is a chromosome? ☑
2) What does diploid mean? What is the diploid number for a human body cell? ☑
3) Give one difference between a molecule of DNA and a molecule of RNA. ☐
4) Name the two main stages of protein synthesis. ☐

Reproduction and Cell Division (p.56-57) ☐

5) a) Name the type of cell division used in asexual reproduction.
   b) Apart from asexual reproduction, what else is this type of cell division used for? ☑
6) Name the type of cell division that creates gametes. Where does it take place in humans? ☑

Reproduction, Fertilisation and Germination in Plants (p.58-61) ☐

7) Name the male and female reproductive parts of a flower. ☑
8) What is pollination? ☐
9) What is fertilisation? How does the pollen get from the stigma to the ovary? ☑
10) What conditions are needed for seed germination?
    Outline an experiment you could do to investigate these conditions. ☑
11) Give an example of a plant that reproduces asexually and briefly describe how it happens. ☐
12) Describe how to make plant clones from cuttings. ☑

Male and Female Reproductive Systems and Hormones (p.62-63) ☑

13) Where are sperm made? Where are ova made? ☑
14) What secondary sexual characteristics does testosterone trigger in males? ☑
15) Sketch a timeline of the 28-day menstrual cycle. Label the four stages of the cycle. ☐
16) Name the hormone that causes an egg to mature in an ovary. ☑
17) What is the function of the amniotic fluid in pregnancy? ☑

Inheritance and Genetic Diagrams (p.64-66) ☐

18) What does it mean if you are homozygous for a particular trait? ☐
19) What are codominant alleles? ☐
20) How are carriers shown on a family pedigree? ☐
21) Draw a genetic diagram showing that there's an equal chance of a baby being a boy or a girl. ☐

Variation, Evolution, Mutations and Antibiotic Resistance (p.67-69) ☐

22) List four features of animals which aren't affected at all by their environment, and three which are. ☑
23) Who proposed the theory of evolution by natural selection? ☐
24) Explain what is meant by natural selection. ☐
25) What is a mutation? ☐
26) What is a 'superbug'? ☐

Ecosystems and Biodiversity

This is where the <u>fun</u> starts. Studying <u>ecology</u> gives you the chance to <u>rummage around</u> in bushes, get your hands <u>dirty</u> and look at some <u>real organisms</u>, living in the <u>wild</u>. Hold on to your hats folks...

You Need to Learn Some Definitions to Get You Started

Habitat — The <u>place</u> where an organism <u>lives</u>, e.g. a rocky shore or a field.
Population — <u>All</u> the organisms of <u>one species</u> in a <u>habitat</u>.
Community — All the <u>different species</u> in a habitat.
Ecosystem — All the <u>organisms</u> living in a <u>particular area</u> and all the <u>non-living</u> (abiotic) <u>conditions</u>, e.g. temperature, climate, soil-type.

Biodiversity is all About the Variety of Life in an Area

Biodiversity is the variety of different species of organisms on Earth, or within an ecosystem.

1) <u>High</u> biodiversity is important. It makes sure that <u>ecosystems</u> are <u>stable</u> because different species depend on each other for things like <u>shelter</u> and <u>food</u>. Different species can also help to maintain the right <u>physical environment</u> for each other (e.g. the acidity of the soil).
2) Lots of human actions, including <u>deforestation</u> (see p.79), <u>pollution</u> (p.77 and 79), as well as <u>global warming</u> (p.78) are reducing biodiversity.

Paper 2

Environmental Changes Affect Communities in Different Ways

The <u>environment</u> in which plants and animals live <u>changes all the time</u>. These changes are caused by <u>abiotic</u> (non-living) and <u>biotic</u> (living) factors and affect communities in different ways — for some species <u>population size</u> may <u>increase</u>, for others it may <u>decrease</u>, or the <u>distribution</u> of populations (where they live) may change. Here are some <u>examples</u> of the effects of changes in <u>abiotic</u> and <u>biotic</u> factors:

Abiotic Factors Affect Communities...

1) <u>Environmental conditions</u> — e.g. the distribution of <u>bird species</u> in Germany appears to be changing because of a <u>rise</u> in average <u>temperature</u>. Other environmental conditions that affect the abundance and distribution of organisms include <u>light intensity</u> (plants only), <u>moisture level</u> and <u>soil pH</u>.
2) <u>Toxic chemicals</u> — e.g. chemical pesticides or fertilisers. Pesticides can <u>build up</u> in food chains through <u>bioaccumulation</u> — this is where, at each stage of the food chain, concentration of the pesticide increases, so <u>organisms</u> at the <u>top</u> of the chain receive a <u>toxic dose</u>. <u>Excess fertilisers</u> released into <u>lakes</u> and <u>ponds</u> cause <u>eutrophication</u> (see p.79) which leads to the <u>death</u> of organisms (e.g. fish).

... and so do Biotic Factors

1) <u>Availability of food</u> — e.g. in a <u>bumper year</u> for <u>berries</u>, the population of <u>blackbirds</u> might <u>increase</u> because there'll be <u>enough food</u> for all of them, so they're more likely to <u>survive</u> and <u>reproduce</u>.
2) <u>Number of predators</u> — e.g. if the <u>number of lions</u> (predator) <u>decreases</u> then the number of <u>gazelles</u> (prey) might <u>increase</u> because <u>fewer</u> of them will be <u>eaten</u> by the lions.
3) <u>Competition</u> — organisms <u>compete with other species</u> (and members of their own species) for the <u>same resources</u>. E.g. <u>plants</u> need things like <u>light</u>, <u>space</u>, <u>water</u> and <u>minerals</u> from the soil. Animals compete for things like <u>space</u> (territory), <u>shelter</u>, <u>food</u>, <u>water</u> and <u>mates</u>.

Revision — an abiotic factor causing stress in my community...

Organisms like everything to be just right — temperature, light, food... I'd never get away with being that fussy.

Q1   Give two abiotic factors that could affect the population size of a species in an ecosystem.   [2 marks]

Using Quadrats

Time to put some <u>ecology investigations</u> into action now...

Use a Quadrat to Study The Population Size of Small Organisms

A <u>quadrat</u> is a <u>square</u> frame enclosing a <u>known area</u>, e.g. 1 m². To compare the <u>population size</u> of an organism in <u>two sample areas</u> just follow these simple steps:

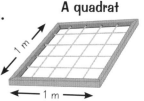

A quadrat

1) Place a <u>1 m² quadrat</u> on the ground at a <u>random point</u> within the <u>first</u> sample area. You could do this by dividing the sample area into a grid and using a random number generator to pick coordinates to place your quadrats at. This will help to make sure the results you get are <u>representative</u> of the <u>whole sample area</u>.

2) <u>Count</u> all the organisms you're interested in <u>within</u> the quadrat.

3) <u>Repeat</u> steps 1 and 2 lots of times.

4) <u>Work out</u> the <u>mean</u> number of organisms per quadrat within the first sample area.

5) <u>Repeat</u> steps 1 to 4 in the <u>second</u> sample area.

6) Finally <u>compare</u> the two means. E.g. you might find a mean of 2 daisies per m² in one area, and 22 daisies per m² (lots more) in another area.

$$\text{Mean} = \frac{\text{total number of organisms}}{\text{number of quadrats}}$$

Estimate Population Size by Scaling Up from a Small Sample Area

To work out the <u>population size</u> of an organism in one sample area you need to work out the <u>mean number of organisms per m²</u> (if your quadrat has an area of 1 m², this is the same as the mean number of organisms per quadrat, worked out above). Then just <u>multiply the mean</u> by the <u>total area</u> of the habitat:

> Students used 0.5 m² quadrats to randomly sample daisies in a field. They found a mean of 10 daisies per quadrat. The field's area was 800 m². Estimate the population of daisies in the field.
>
> 1) Work out the <u>mean number of organisms per m²</u>.   1 ÷ 0.5 = 2   2 × 10 = 20 daisies per m²
> 2) Multiply the <u>mean per m²</u> by the <u>total area</u> (in m²) of the habitat.   20 × 800 = **16 000 daisies in the field**

Use Belt Transects to Study Distribution Across a Habitat

Sometimes <u>abiotic factors</u> will <u>change across a habitat</u>. You can use quadrats to help find out how organisms (like plants) are <u>distributed</u> across a habitat. For example, how a species becomes <u>more or less common</u> as you move from an area of <u>shade</u> (near a hedge at the edge of a field) to an area of full sun (the middle of the field). The quadrats are laid out along a <u>line</u>, forming a <u>belt transect</u>:

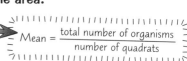

tape measure

1) <u>Mark out a line</u> in the area you want to study, e.g. from the hedge to the middle of the field.

2) Then <u>collect data</u> along the line using <u>quadrats</u> placed <u>next to</u> each other. If your transect is <u>quite long</u>, you could place the quadrats at <u>regular intervals</u> (e.g. every 2 metres) instead. <u>Count</u> all the organisms of the species you're interested in, or <u>estimate percentage cover</u> (estimating the <u>percentage area</u> of a quadrat covered by a particular type of organism).

quadrat 1

3) You could also <u>record</u> other data, such as the <u>mean height</u> of the plants you're counting or the <u>abiotic factors</u> in each quadrat (e.g. you could use a <u>light meter</u> to measure the light intensity).

4) <u>Repeat</u> steps 1-3 several times, then find the <u>mean</u> number of organisms or mean percentage cover for <u>each quadrat</u>.

5) Plot graphs to see if the <u>changing abiotic factor</u> is <u>correlated</u> with a change in the <u>distribution</u> of the species you're studying.

You can measure biodiversity in an area by recording the number of different species that are present, and using quadrats to work out how many organisms of each species there are.

Drat, drat, and double drat — my favourite use of quadrats...

Unless you're doing a belt transect, it's key that you put your quadrat down in a random place before you start counting.

Q1   A field was randomly sampled for buttercups using 0.25 m² quadrats. The field had an area of 1200 m². A mean of 0.75 buttercups were found per quadrat. Estimate the total population of buttercups.   [2 marks]

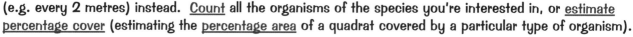

Paper 2

Section 8 — Ecology and the Environment

Pyramids of Number, Biomass and Energy

OK, I'll level with you. This isn't the most <u>interesting</u> page in the world, but hey — life's like that.
At least you're not being eaten by a load of <u>rabbits</u>...

Food Chains Show What's Eaten by What in an Ecosystem

1) <u>Food chains</u> always start with a <u>producer</u>, e.g. a plant.
Producers <u>make</u> (produce) <u>their own food</u> using energy from the Sun.

2) Producers are eaten by <u>primary consumers</u>.
Primary consumers are then eaten by <u>secondary consumers</u>
and secondary consumers are eaten by <u>tertiary consumers</u>.

3) All these organisms eventually die and get eaten by <u>decomposers</u>, e.g.
bacteria. Decomposers <u>break down</u> (decompose) <u>dead material</u> and <u>waste</u>.

4) Each <u>stage</u> (e.g. producers, primary consumers) is called a <u>trophic level</u>.

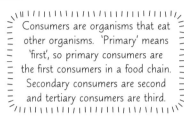
Consumers are organisms that eat other organisms. 'Primary' means 'first', so primary consumers are the first consumers in a food chain. Secondary consumers are second and tertiary consumers are third.

Here's an <u>example</u> of a food chain:

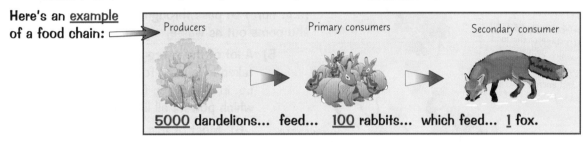

Producers — Primary consumers — Secondary consumer

<u>5000</u> dandelions... feed... <u>100</u> rabbits... which feed... <u>1</u> fox.

You Need to Understand Pyramids of Numbers

Here's a <u>pyramid of numbers</u> for the food chain above.

1) Each bar on a pyramid of numbers shows the <u>number of organisms</u> at that stage of the food chain.

2) So the '<u>dandelions</u>' bar on this pyramid would need to be <u>longer</u> than the '<u>rabbits</u>' bar, which in turn should be <u>longer</u> than the '<u>fox</u>' bar.

Secondary consumer → 1 fox
Primary consumers → 100 rabbits
Producers → 5000 dandelions

3) <u>Dandelions</u> go at the <u>bottom</u> because they're at the bottom of the food chain.

4) This is a <u>typical pyramid of numbers</u>, where every time you go up a <u>trophic level</u>, the number of organisms goes <u>down</u>. This is because it takes a <u>lot</u> of food from the level below to keep one animal alive.

5) There are cases where a number pyramid is <u>not a pyramid at all</u>. For example 1 fox may feed 500 fleas.

You Have to Understand Pyramids of Biomass Too

1) Each bar on a <u>pyramid of biomass</u> shows the <u>mass of living material</u> at that stage of the food chain — basically how much all the organisms at each level would '<u>weigh</u>' if you put them <u>all together</u>.

2) So the one fox would have a <u>big biomass</u> and the <u>hundreds of fleas</u> would have a <u>very small biomass</u>. Biomass pyramids are <u>practically always the right shape</u>.

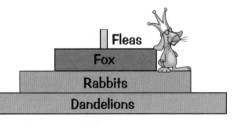
Fleas
Fox
Rabbits
Dandelions

Pyramids of Energy Transfer Are Always Pyramid-Shaped

1) <u>Pyramids of energy</u> show the <u>energy</u> transferred to each trophic level in a food chain.
E.g. when a rabbit eats dandelions it gets energy, which the dandelions got from the Sun.

2) Pyramids of energy transfer are <u>always the right shape</u> — a nice, regular pyramid.

Constructing pyramids is a breeze — just ask the Egyptians...

When it comes to interpreting a pyramid, make sure you know if it's a pyramid of number, biomass or energy transfer.

Q1 What does each bar on a pyramid of biomass represent? [1 mark]

Section 8 — Ecology and the Environment

Energy Transfer and Food Webs

Some organisms get their energy from the Sun. Some get it from other organisms. How very friendly. Yeah right.

Energy is Transferred Along a Food Chain

1) Energy from the Sun is the source of energy for nearly all life on Earth.

2) Plants use energy from the Sun to make food during photosynthesis. This energy then works its way through the food chain as animals eat the plants and each other.

3) Not all the energy that's available to the organisms in a trophic level is passed on to the next trophic level — around 90% of the energy is lost in various ways.

4) Some parts of food, e.g. roots or bones, aren't eaten by organisms so the energy isn't taken in. Some parts of food are indigestible (e.g. fibre) so pass through organisms and come out as waste, e.g. faeces.

5) A lot of the energy that does get taken in is used for staying alive, i.e. in respiration (see page 29), which powers all life processes.

6) Most of this energy is eventually transferred to the surroundings by heat.

7) Only around 10% of the total energy available becomes biomass, i.e. it's stored or used for growth.

8) This is the energy that's transferred from one trophic level to the next.

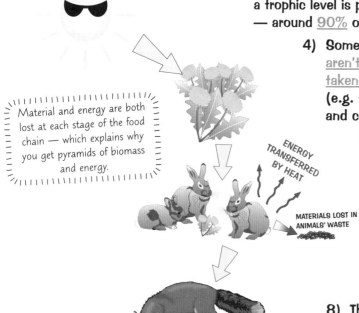

Material and energy are both lost at each stage of the food chain — which explains why you get pyramids of biomass and energy.

ENERGY TRANSFERRED BY HEAT

MATERIALS LOST IN ANIMALS' WASTE

Food Webs Show How Food Chains are Linked

1) There are many different species within an environment — which means lots of different possible food chains. You can draw a food web to show them.

2) All the species in a food web are interdependent, which means if one species changes, it affects all the others. For example, in the food web on the right, if lots of water spiders died, then:

- There would be less food for the frogs, so their numbers might decrease.

- The number of mayfly larvae might increase since the water spiders wouldn't be eating them.

- The diving beetles wouldn't be competing with the water spiders for food, so their numbers might increase.

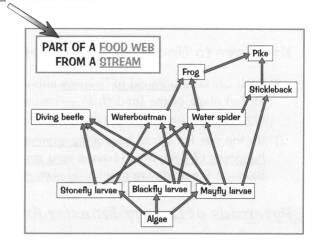

PART OF A FOOD WEB FROM A STREAM

Food webs — nothing to do with ordering pizza online, I'm afraid...

Food webs are handy for looking at relationships between individual species. Unfortunately you hardly ever see simple food webs in the real world — they're normally tangled together and interlinked like a bowl of spaghetti.

Q1 Look at the following food chain for a particular area:
grass → grasshopper → rat → snake
All of the rats in the area are killed. Explain two effects that this could have on the food chain. [4 marks]

The Carbon Cycle

Substances like <u>carbon</u> and <u>nitrogen</u> are <u>essential</u> to <u>life</u> on Earth. Luckily for us, they flow through the Earth's <u>ecosystems</u> in <u>cycles</u>, meaning that we (and other organisms) can <u>reuse them</u> over and over again — splendid.

Materials are Constantly Recycled in an Ecosystem

1) Remember, an <u>ecosystem</u> is a <u>community</u> of <u>organisms</u> living in an area, as well as all the <u>non-living</u> (abiotic) conditions, e.g. soil quality, availability of water, temperature. There's more on these on p.71.

2) Materials that organisms need to survive, such as <u>carbon</u> and <u>nitrogen</u> (see next page) are <u>recycled</u> through <u>both</u> the <u>biotic</u> and <u>abiotic</u> components of ecosystems.

3) This means they pass through both <u>living organisms</u> (the biotic components of an ecosystem) and things like the <u>air</u>, <u>rocks</u> and <u>soil</u> (abiotic components of an ecosystem) in a <u>continuous cycle</u>.

The Carbon Cycle Shows How Carbon is Recycled

<u>Carbon</u> is an important element in the materials that living things are made from. But there's only a <u>fixed amount</u> of carbon in the world. This means it's constantly <u>recycled</u>:

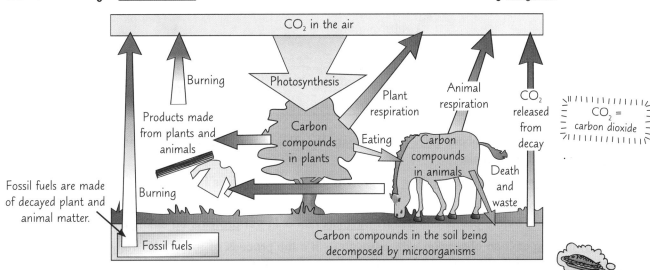

This diagram isn't half as bad as it looks. <u>Learn</u> these important points:

1) There's only <u>one arrow</u> going <u>down</u> from <u>CO$_2$</u> in the air. The whole thing is 'powered' by <u>photosynthesis</u> (see page 20). Green <u>plants</u> use the carbon from <u>CO$_2$</u> to make <u>carbohydrates</u>, <u>lipids</u> and <u>proteins</u>.

2) <u>Eating</u> passes the carbon compounds in the plant along to <u>animals</u> in a food chain or web (p.73-74).

3) <u>Respiration</u> (see page 29) by living plants and animals <u>releases CO$_2$</u> back into the <u>air</u>.

4) Plants and animals eventually <u>die</u> and <u>decompose</u>, or are killed and turned into <u>useful products</u>.

5) When plants and animals decompose they're broken down by microorganisms, such as <u>bacteria</u> and <u>fungi</u>. These microorganisms are known as <u>decomposers</u> and they release <u>enzymes</u>, which <u>catalyse</u> the breakdown of dead material into <u>smaller molecules</u>. Decomposers <u>release CO$_2$</u> back into the air by <u>respiration</u> as they break down the material.

6) Some useful plant and animal <u>products</u>, e.g. wood and fossil fuels, are <u>burned</u> (<u>combustion</u>). This also releases <u>CO$_2$</u> back into the air.

7) <u>Decomposition</u> of materials means that <u>habitats</u> can be <u>maintained</u> for the organisms that live there, e.g. <u>nutrients</u> are <u>returned</u> to the soil and <u>waste material</u> (such as dead leaves) doesn't just <u>pile up</u>.

The Carbon Cycle — a great gift for any bike enthusiast...

Carbon atoms are very important — they're found in plants, animals, your petrol tank and on your burnt toast.

Q1   Suggest two reasons why chopping down trees can increase the concentration of CO$_2$ in the air.   [2 marks]

The Nitrogen Cycle

Nitrogen, just like carbon, is constantly being <u>recycled</u>. So the nitrogen in your proteins might once have been in the <u>air</u>. And before that it might have been in a <u>plant</u>. Or even in some <u>horse wee</u>. Nice.

Nitrogen is Recycled in the Nitrogen Cycle

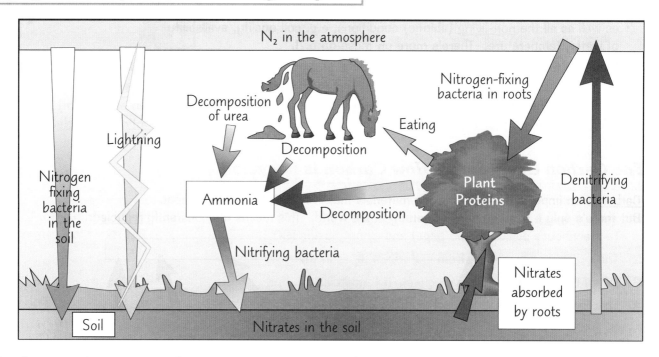

1) The <u>atmosphere</u> contains about <u>78% nitrogen gas</u>, N_2. This is <u>very unreactive</u> and so it can't be used <u>directly</u> by plants or animals.

2) <u>Nitrogen</u> is <u>needed</u> for making <u>proteins</u> for growth, so living organisms have to get it somehow.

3) Plants get their nitrogen from the <u>soil</u>, so nitrogen in the air has to be turned into <u>nitrogen compounds</u> (such as nitrates) before plants can use it. <u>Animals</u> can only get <u>proteins</u> by eating plants (or each other).

4) <u>Nitrogen fixation</u> isn't an obsession with nitrogen — it's the process of turning <u>N_2 from the air</u> into <u>nitrogen compounds</u> in the soil which <u>plants can use</u>. There are <u>two main ways</u> that this happens:

    a) <u>LIGHTNING</u> — there's so much <u>energy</u> in a bolt of lightning that it's enough to make nitrogen <u>react with oxygen</u> in the air to give nitrates.

    b) <u>NITROGEN-FIXING BACTERIA</u> in soil and the roots of some plants (see below).

> When ammonia is dissolved in water, ammonium ions are formed.

5) There are <u>four</u> different types of <u>bacteria</u> involved in the nitrogen cycle:

    a) <u>DECOMPOSERS</u> — break down <u>proteins</u> (in rotting plants and animals) and <u>urea</u> (in animal waste) and turn them into <u>ammonia</u> (a nitrogen compound). This forms <u>ammonium ions</u> in the soil.

    b) <u>NITRIFYING BACTERIA</u> — turn <u>ammonium ions</u> in decaying matter into <u>nitrates</u> (<u>nitrification</u>).

    c) <u>NITROGEN-FIXING BACTERIA</u> — turn <u>atmospheric N_2</u> into <u>nitrogen compounds</u> that plants can use.

    d) <u>DENITRIFYING BACTERIA</u> — turn <u>nitrates</u> back into <u>N_2 gas</u>. This is of no benefit to living organisms.

Some of these bacteria live in the <u>soil</u> and some of them live in <u>nodules</u> on plant roots.

It's the cyyyycle of liiiiife...

Bacteria do all the hard work in the nitrogen cycle. Aided by a bolt or two of lightning. Nitrogen is vital to living things, because it's found in proteins, which are needed for things like enzymes. Make sure you learn this page.

Q1   Outline the role of lightning in the nitrogen cycle.   [1 mark]

Q2   Describe how the nitrogen compounds in dead leaves are turned into nitrates in the soil.   [2 marks]

Air Pollution

Water, carbon and nitrogen all pass through the air as an essential part of natural cycles. But air pollutants can cause lots of problems when they're released into the atmosphere — especially when we put them there.

Carbon Monoxide is Poisonous

1) When fossil fuels are burnt without enough air supply they produce the gas carbon monoxide (CO).

2) It's a poisonous gas. If it combines with haemoglobin in red blood cells, it prevents them from carrying oxygen.

3) Carbon monoxide's mostly released in car emissions. Most modern cars are fitted with catalytic converters that turn the carbon monoxide into carbon dioxide, decreasing the amount of CO that's released into the atmosphere.

Acid Rain is Caused by Sulfur Dioxide

1) Burning fossil fuels releases harmful gases like CO_2 (a greenhouse gas, see next page) and sulfur dioxide (SO_2).

2) The sulfur dioxide comes from sulfur impurities in the fossil fuels.

3) When this gas mixes with rain clouds it forms dilute sulfuric acid.

4) This then falls as acid rain.

5) Internal combustion engines in cars and power stations are the main causes of acid rain.

Acid rain is also caused by nitrogen oxides that are produced by burning fossil fuels.

sulfur dioxide → → Clean Cloud → Acid Cloud → Acid Rain

Acid Rain Kills Fish and Trees

1) Acid rain can cause a lake to become more acidic. This has a severe effect on the lake's ecosystem. Many organisms are sensitive to changes in pH and can't survive in more acidic conditions. Many plants and animals die.

2) Acid rain can kill trees. The acid damages leaves and releases toxic substances from the soil, making it hard for the trees to take up nutrients.

It's raining, it's pouring — quick, cover the rhododendron...

Exam questions on this topic might ask you to describe the effects of air pollution. Or they may give you a graph or table to interpret — in which case you'll have to apply your knowledge. Either way, you'll need to learn all the facts on this page. Try covering up the page and jotting down everything you can remember. What are you waiting for...

Q1   Explain why sulfur dioxide is considered to be a pollutant.   [3 marks]

The Greenhouse Effect

The <u>greenhouse effect</u> is always in the news. We need it, since it makes Earth a suitable temperature for living on. But unfortunately it's starting to trap more heat than is necessary.

Greenhouse Gases Trap Energy from the Sun

1) The <u>temperature</u> of the Earth is a <u>balance</u> between the energy it gets from the Sun and the energy it radiates back out into space.

2) Gases in the <u>atmosphere</u> absorb most of the heat that would normally be radiated out into space, and re-radiate it in all directions (including back towards the Earth). This is the <u>greenhouse effect</u>.

3) If this didn't happen, then at night there'd be nothing to keep any energy <u>in</u>, and we'd quickly get <u>very cold</u> indeed.

4) There are several different gases in the atmosphere that help keep the <u>energy in</u>. They're called "<u>greenhouse gases</u>" (oddly enough) and they include <u>water vapour</u>, <u>carbon dioxide</u> and <u>methane</u>.

This is what happens in a greenhouse. The Sun shines in, and the glass helps keeps some of the energy in.

5) <u>Human beings</u> are <u>increasing</u> the amount of <u>carbon dioxide</u> in the atmosphere (see below). We're also increasing levels of other gases that can act as greenhouse gases, e.g. <u>CFCs</u> and <u>nitrous oxide</u> (again, see below). This has <u>enhanced</u> the <u>greenhouse effect</u>.

6) As a result of all this, the Earth is <u>heating up</u> — this is <u>global warming</u>. Global warming is a type of <u>climate change</u> and causes other types of climate change, e.g. changing rainfall patterns. Climate change could lead to things like <u>extreme weather</u>, and <u>rising sea levels</u> and <u>flooding</u> due to the <u>polar ice caps</u> <u>melting</u>. This could cause <u>habitat loss</u>, and could affect <u>food webs</u> and <u>crop growth</u>.

Human Activity Produces Lots of Greenhouse Gases

CARBON DIOXIDE

1) <u>Humans</u> release <u>carbon dioxide</u> into the atmosphere all the time as part of our <u>everyday lives</u> — in <u>car exhausts</u>, <u>industrial processes</u>, as we <u>burn fossil fuels</u> etc.

2) People around the world are also <u>cutting down</u> large areas of forest (<u>deforestation</u>) for <u>timber</u> and to clear land for <u>farming</u> — and this activity affects the <u>level of carbon dioxide</u> in the <u>atmosphere</u> (see next page).

METHANE

1) <u>Methane gas</u> is produced <u>naturally</u> from various sources, e.g. <u>rotting plants</u> in <u>marshland</u>.

2) However, two 'man-made' sources of methane are <u>on the increase</u>: <u>rice growing</u> and <u>cattle rearing</u> — it's the cows' "pumping" that's the problem, believe it or not.

NITROUS OXIDE

1) <u>Nitrous oxide</u> is released naturally by <u>bacteria</u> in <u>soils</u> and the <u>ocean</u>.

2) A lot more is released from soils after <u>fertiliser</u> is used.

3) It's also released from <u>vehicle engines</u> and industry.

CFCs

1) <u>CFCs</u> are <u>man-made</u> chemicals that were once used in <u>aerosol sprays</u> (e.g. deodorant) and <u>fridges</u>. They're really <u>powerful</u> greenhouse gases.

2) Most countries have agreed <u>not to produce them</u> any more because they also damage the <u>ozone layer</u> that prevents UV radiation from reaching the Earth.

3) But some CFCs still remain and get released, e.g. by <u>leaks</u> from old fridges.

Methane is a stinky problem but an important one...

Global warming is rarely out of the news. There's a consensus among scientists that it's happening and that human activity has caused most of the recent warming. But, they don't know exactly what the effects will be.

Q1   Name three greenhouse gases.   [3 marks]

Water Pollution and Deforestation

I'm sorry to bring so much gloom in such a short space, but here are a couple more environmental problems...

Fertilisers Can Leach into Water and Cause Eutrophication

You might think fertiliser would be a good thing for the environment because it makes plants grow faster. Unfortunately it causes big problems when it ends up in lakes and rivers — here's how...

1) Nitrates and phosphates are put onto fields as mineral fertilisers.
2) If too much fertiliser is applied and it rains afterwards, nitrates are easily leached (washed through the soil) into rivers and lakes.
3) The result is eutrophication, which can cause serious damage to river and lake ecosystems:

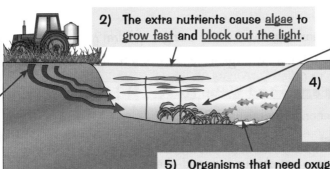

1) Fertilisers enter the water, adding extra nutrients (nitrates and phosphates).

2) The extra nutrients cause algae to grow fast and block out the light.

3) Plants can't photosynthesise due to lack of light and start to die.

4) With more food available, microorganisms that feed on dead plants increase in number and deplete (use up) all the oxygen in the water.

5) Organisms that need oxygen (e.g. fish) die.

4) Another cause of eutrophication is pollution by sewage. Sewage contains lots of phosphates from detergents, e.g. washing powder. It also contains nitrates from urine and faeces.
5) These extra nutrients cause eutrophication in the same way that fertilisers do.

Deforestation Affects The Soil, Evapotranspiration and Carbon Cycle

Deforestation is bad. Chop down all the trees, and the animals and insects that lived there will disappear too. But there are some other nasty effects that you need to know about...

LEACHING

- Trees take up nutrients from the soil before they can be washed away (leached) by rain, but return them to the soil when leaves die.
- When trees are removed nutrients get leached away, but don't get replaced, leaving infertile soil.

SOIL EROSION

- Tree roots hold the soil together.
- When trees are removed, soil can be washed away by the rain (eroded) leaving infertile ground.

DISTURBING THE BALANCE OF CARBON DIOXIDE AND OXYGEN

- Forests take up CO_2 by photosynthesis, store it in wood, and slowly release it when they decompose (microorganisms feeding on bits of dead wood release CO_2 as a waste product of respiration).
- When trees are cut down and burnt, the stored carbon is released at once as CO_2. This disturbs the carbon cycle and contributes to global warming (see the previous page).
- Fewer trees in the forest also means that less photosynthesis takes place, releasing less oxygen. This causes the oxygen level in the atmosphere to drop.

DISTURBING EVAPOTRANSPIRATION

- Evapotranspiration includes both the processes of water evaporating from the Earth's surface and from plant transpiration (page 26).
- This water falls back to the Earth as rain (or hail or snow).
- So, when trees are cut down, evapotranspiration is reduced, which can make the local climate drier.

Paper 2

Bet you never knew trees were so useful...

Trees remove CO_2 from the atmosphere as they grow — but once they die and decompose, the CO_2 is released. But if the carbon gets stored in wood products, it is permanently removed from the atmosphere.

Q1   Give one human action that can result in eutrophication.   [1 mark]

Revision Questions for Section 8

You've battled to the end of Section 8, but don't stop now — pit yourself against these questions to claim glory.

- Try these questions and tick off each one when you get it right.
- When you've done all the questions for a topic and are completely happy with it, tick off the topic.

Ecosystems, Biodiversity and Using Quadrats (p.71-72) ☑

1) Define the following:
   a) a habitat
   b) a population
   c) an ecosystem
   d) biodiversity ☑
2) How could you estimate a population size in a habitat using a quadrat? ☑
3) How could you investigate the distribution of organisms across a habitat using quadrats? ☑

Pyramids, Energy Transfer and Food Webs (p.73-74) ☐

4) What's a producer? What's a secondary consumer? ☑
5) Give an example of a decomposer. ☑
6) Explain why pyramids of number are not always pyramid-shaped. ☑
7) What is the source of all the energy in a typical food chain? ☑
8) Give two reasons why energy is lost between trophic levels. ☑
9) Approximately how much energy is passed on to the next trophic level? ☑
10) What does a food web show? ☑

The Carbon Cycle and the Nitrogen Cycle (p.75-76) ☐

11) How does carbon enter the carbon cycle from the air? ☑
12) Give two ways that carbon can enter the air from dead plants and animals. ☑
13) What role do decomposers play in the nitrogen cycle? ☑
14) What role do nitrogen-fixing bacteria play in the nitrogen cycle? ☑

Pollution, The Greenhouse Effect and Deforestation (p.77-79) ☐

15) Name a gas that causes acid rain. Where does it come from? ☑
16) How does acid rain affect lakes and trees? ☑
17) How does the greenhouse effect work? ☑
18) What is the effect of increasing the concentration of greenhouse gases in the atmosphere? ☑
19) Give two man-made sources of methane. ☑
20) Explain how fertilisers can cause eutrophication. ☑
21) Describe four effects of deforestation. ☑

Increasing Crop Yields

A plant's rate of photosynthesis is affected by the amount of light, the amount of carbon dioxide (CO_2) and the temperature (see page 21). Since plants have to photosynthesise in order to make food for themselves and grow, these three factors need to be carefully controlled in order to maximise crop yield.

You Can Artificially Create the Ideal Conditions for Photosynthesis

Photosynthesis can be helped along by artificially creating the ideal conditions in glasshouses (big greenhouses to you and me) or polytunnels (big tube-like structures made from polythene).

1) Keeping plants enclosed in a glasshouse makes it easier to keep them free from pests and diseases.

2) It also helps farmers to control the water supplied to their crops.

3) Commercial farmers often supply artificial light after the Sun goes down to give their plants more time to photosynthesise.

4) Glasshouses trap the Sun's heat to keep the plants warm. In winter, a farmer might also use a heater to help keep the temperature at the ideal level.

5) Farmers can also increase the level of carbon dioxide in glasshouses, e.g. by using a paraffin heater to heat the place. As the paraffin burns, it makes carbon dioxide as a by-product.

6) By increasing the temperature and CO_2 concentration, as well as the amount of light available, a farmer can increase the rate of photosynthesis for his or her plants. This means the plants will grow bigger and faster — and crop yields will be higher.

Fertilisers Are Used to Ensure the Crops Have Enough Minerals

1) Plants need certain minerals, e.g. nitrogen, potassium and phosphorus, so they can make important compounds like proteins.

2) If plants don't get enough of these minerals, their growth and life processes are affected.

3) Sometimes these minerals are missing from the soil because they've been used up by a previous crop.

4) Farmers use fertilisers to replace these missing minerals or provide more of them. This helps to increase the crop yield.

Pest Control Stops Pests Eating Crops

1) Pests include microorganisms, insects and mammals (e.g. rats). Pests that feed on crops are killed using various methods of pest control. This means fewer plants are damaged or destroyed, increasing crop yield.

2) Pesticides are a form of chemical pest control. They're often poisonous to humans, so they must be used carefully to keep the amount of pesticide in food below a safe level. Some pesticides also harm other wildlife.

3) Biological control is an alternative to using pesticides. It means using other organisms to reduce the numbers of pests, either by encouraging wild organisms or adding new ones.

4) The helpful organisms could be predators (e.g. ladybirds eat aphids), parasites (e.g. some flies lay their eggs on slugs, eventually killing them), or disease-causing (e.g. bacteria that affect caterpillars).

5) Biological control can have a longer-lasting effect than spraying pesticides, and be less harmful to wildlife. But introducing new organisms can cause problems — e.g. cane toads were introduced to Australia to eat beetles, but they are now a major pest themselves because they poison the native species that eat them.

People who live in glasshouses — will get very warm...

Right. Now you know exactly what to do to increase crop yields. Excellent. With all this new-found knowledge you could take over the world — or at least help Gran with her veggie patch...

Q1　　Explain why increasing the temperature and carbon dioxide concentration in a glasshouse can help to increase the yield of a crop.

[2 marks]

Bacteria and Making Yoghurt

Lots of microorganisms are used to produce food, including <u>bacteria</u>. You need to know how <u>yoghurt</u> is produced, and how giant <u>fermenters</u> are used for industrial-scale production of microbial products.

Bacteria Ferment Milk to Produce Yoghurt

<u>Fermentation</u> is when <u>microorganisms</u> break sugars down to release energy — usually by <u>anaerobic respiration</u>. <u>Yoghurt</u> is basically <u>fermented milk</u>. Here's how it's made...

1) The <u>equipment</u> is <u>sterilised</u> to kill off any unwanted microorganisms.
2) The milk is <u>pasteurised</u> (heated up to 72 °C for 15 seconds) — again to kill any harmful microorganisms. Then the milk's <u>cooled</u>.
3) <u>Lactobacillus</u> bacteria are added, and the mixture is <u>incubated</u> (heated to about 40 °C) in a vessel called a <u>fermenter</u> (see below).
4) The bacteria ferment the <u>lactose sugar</u> in the milk to form <u>lactic acid</u>.
5) Lactic acid causes the milk to <u>clot</u>, and <u>solidify</u> into <u>yoghurt</u>.
6) Finally, <u>flavours</u> (e.g. fruit) and <u>colours</u> are sometimes added and the yoghurt is <u>packaged</u>.

Microorganisms are Grown in Fermenters

1) <u>Microorganisms</u> (like bacteria) can be used to make really <u>useful stuff</u>, e.g. penicillin or insulin (see p.86).
2) <u>In industry</u>, microorganisms are grown in large containers called <u>fermenters</u>. The fermenter is full of liquid '<u>culture medium</u>' in which microorganisms can grow and reproduce.
3) The conditions inside the fermentation vessels are kept at the <u>optimum</u> (best) levels <u>for growth</u> — this means the <u>yield</u> of <u>products</u> from the microorganisms can be <u>as big as possible</u>.

Here's a bit about how fermenters work:

<u>Nutrients</u> needed by the microorganisms for <u>growth</u> are provided in the liquid <u>culture medium</u>.

The <u>pH</u> is monitored and kept at the <u>optimum level</u> for the microorganisms' <u>enzymes</u> to work <u>efficiently</u>. This keeps the <u>rate of reaction</u> and product yield as high as possible.

The <u>temperature</u> is also monitored and kept at an <u>optimum level</u>. A <u>water-cooled</u> jacket makes sure it doesn't get <u>so hot</u> that the enzymes <u>denature</u>.

Nutrients in
Microorganisms in
Exhaust gases out
pH probe
Water out
Water-cooled jacket
Paddles to stir the mixture
Temperature recorder
Water in
Air in   Product out

Microorganisms are kept in <u>contact</u> with <u>fresh medium</u> by <u>paddles</u> that <u>circulate</u> (or <u>agitate</u>) the medium around the vessel. This <u>increases</u> the product yield because microorganisms can <u>always access</u> the <u>nutrients</u> needed for <u>growth</u>.

If the microorganisms need <u>oxygen</u> for <u>respiration</u>, it's added by pumping in sterile air. This <u>increases</u> the product yield because microorganisms can always <u>respire</u> to provide the <u>energy</u> for <u>growth</u>.

Vessels are <u>sterilised</u> between uses with <u>superheated steam</u> that kills <u>unwanted microbes</u>. Having <u>aseptic</u> conditions <u>increases</u> the product yield because the microorganisms <u>aren't competing</u> with other organisms. It also means that the product doesn't get <u>contaminated</u>.

Pizza, TV and a nice cosy living room — my optimum conditions...

Microorganisms are really useful — not only can you use them to make stuff that other organisms can't, they'll happily grow in a fermenter whether it's hot or cold or blowing a gale outside.

Q1   Explain how the rotating paddles in a fermenter help to increase the product yield. [2 marks]

Yeast and Making Bread

Yeast is a useful microorganism. When it respires aerobically (in the presence of oxygen), it breaks down sugar into CO_2 and water. It's used in baking, where it's mixed into dough to create bubbles of CO_2 that make the dough rise.

We Use Yeast for Making Bread

1) A bread dough is made by mixing yeast with flour, water and a bit of sugar.
2) The dough is then left in a warm place to rise — this happens with the help of the yeast.
3) Enzymes break down the carbohydrates in the flour into sugars.
4) The yeast then uses these sugars in aerobic respiration, producing carbon dioxide.
5) When the oxygen runs out, the yeast switches to anaerobic respiration. This is also known as fermentation, and produces carbon dioxide and alcohol (ethanol).
6) The carbon dioxide produced is trapped in bubbles in the dough.
7) These pockets of gas expand, and the dough begins to rise.
8) The dough is then baked in an oven, where the yeast continues to ferment until the temperature of the dough rises enough to kill the yeast. Any alcohol produced during anaerobic respiration is boiled away.
9) As the yeast dies, the bread stops rising, but pockets are left in the bread where the carbon dioxide was trapped.

The Respiration Rate of Yeast Depends on its Conditions

You can do experiments to investigate how the rate of CO_2 production by yeast during anaerobic respiration changes under different conditions. Here's how to measure the effect of changing temperature:

1) Mix together some sugar, yeast and distilled water, then add the mixture to a test tube.
2) Attach a bung with a tube leading to a second test tube of water.
3) Sealing the two tubes with bungs stops oxygen from getting in, so the yeast will have to start respiring anaerobically.
4) Place the tube containing the yeast mixture in a water bath at a certain temperature.
5) Leave the tube to warm up a bit and then count how many bubbles are produced in a given period of time (e.g. one minute).
6) Calculate the rate of CO_2 production by dividing the number of bubbles produced by the time taken for them to be produced in seconds. This gives an indication of respiration rate.
7) Repeat the experiment with the water bath set at different temperatures.
8) Respiration is controlled by enzymes — so as temperature increases, so should the rate of respiration (up until the optimum temperature, see page 6 for more).

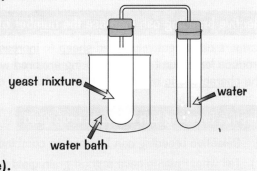

yeast mixture

water

water bath

The example looks at how temperature affects the rate, but the basic idea would be the same whatever variable you were investigating. For example, you could vary the concentration of sugar (but keep the temperature of the water bath the same). You could also alter the experiment to give more accurate results by replacing the second tube with a gas syringe — you'd measure the volume of gas produced instead.

At yeast it's an easy page...

Remember, yeast is a living organism. Its respiration is carried out by enzymes, which are affected by things like temperature and pH. So if you change these conditions, CO_2 production will change too. Ace.

Q1 Explain why bread stops rising whilst being baked in the oven. [2 marks]

Selective Breeding

'Selective breeding' sounds like it has the potential to be a tricky topic, but it's actually dead simple. You take the best plants or animals and breed them together to get the best possible offspring. That's it.

Selective Breeding is Mating the Best Organisms to Get Good Offspring

Organisms are selectively bred to develop the best features, which are things like:

- Maximum yield of meat, milk, grain etc.
- Good health and disease resistance.
- In animals, other qualities like temperament, speed, fertility, good mothering skills, etc.
- In plants, other qualities like attractive flowers, nice smell, etc.

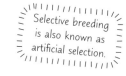

This is the basic process involved in selective breeding:

1) From your existing stock select the ones which have the best characteristics.
2) Breed them with each other.
3) Select the best of the offspring, and breed them together.
4) Continue this process over several generations, and the desirable trait gets stronger and stronger. In farming, this will give the farmer gradually better and better yields.

Selective breeding is also known as artificial selection.

Selective Breeding is Very Useful

Selective breeding can increase the productivity of cows

1) Cows can be selectively bred to produce offspring with, e.g. a high meat yield.
2) First, the animals with characteristics that will increase meat yield (e.g. the largest cows and bulls) are selected and bred together.
3) Next, the offspring with the best characteristics (e.g. the largest) are selected and bred together.
4) If this is continued over several generations, cows with very large meat yields can be produced.
5) Mating cows and bulls naturally can be difficult, so artificial insemination is often used. It's safer for the cow, and it's much quicker and cheaper to transport semen than bulls. The semen can also be used to impregnate multiple cows, and can be stored after the bull has died.

Selective breeding can increase the number of offspring in sheep

Farmers can selectively breed sheep to increase the number of lambs born. Female sheep (ewes) who produce large numbers of offspring are bred with rams whose mothers had large numbers of offspring. The characteristic of having large numbers of offspring is passed on to the next generation.

Selective breeding can increase crop yield

1) Selective breeding can be used to combine two different desirable characteristics.
2) Tall wheat plants have a good grain yield but are easily damaged by wind and rain. Dwarf wheat plants can resist wind and rain but have a lower grain yield.
3) These two types of wheat plant were cross-bred, and the best resulting wheat plants were cross-bred again. This resulted in a new variety of wheat combining the good characteristics — dwarf wheat plants which could resist bad weather and had a high grain yield.

I'll have a roll, a loaf and a french stick — that's selective breading...

Selective breeding's not a new thing. People have been doing it for yonks. That's how we ended up with something like a poodle from a wolf. Somebody thought 'I really like this small, woolly, yappy wolf — I'll breed it with this other one'. And after thousands of generations, we got poodles. Hurrah.

Q1   A farmer who grows green beans lives in an area that experiences a lot of drought. Explain how he could use selective breeding to improve the chances of his bean plants surviving the droughts.   [3 marks]

Fish Farming

We're catching so many wild fish that, if we're not careful, there won't be many left.
A possible solution to this problem is <u>fish farms</u> — big <u>enclosures</u> or <u>tanks</u> where fish are raised for food.
<u>Fish farms</u> rear fish in a controlled way that's designed to produce <u>as many fish as possible</u>.

Fish Can Be Farmed in Cages in the Sea

<u>Salmon farming</u> in Scotland is a good example of this:

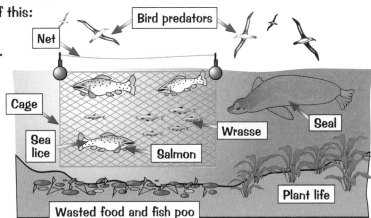

1) The fish are kept in <u>cages</u> in the <u>sea</u> to <u>stop them using as much energy</u> swimming about.

2) The cage also <u>protects</u> them from <u>interspecific predation</u> (being eaten by other animals like birds or seals).

3) They're fed a <u>diet</u> of food pellets that's <u>carefully controlled</u> to <u>maximise</u> the amount of energy they get. The better the <u>quality</u> the food is, the <u>quicker</u> and <u>bigger</u> the fish will grow. (Which is good for us as fish is a great <u>source of protein</u>.)

4) Young fish are reared in <u>special tanks</u> to ensure as many survive as possible.

5) It's important to keep younger fish <u>separate</u> from <u>bigger fish</u>, and to provide <u>regular food</u> — this makes sure that the big fish <u>don't eat the little ones</u>. This is <u>intraspecific predation</u> — where organisms eat individuals of the same species.

6) Fish kept in cages are more prone to <u>disease</u> and <u>parasites</u>. One pest is <u>sea lice</u>, which can be treated with <u>pesticides</u> that kill them. To <u>avoid pollution</u> from chemical pesticides, <u>biological pest control</u> (see p.81) can be used instead, e.g. a small fish called a <u>wrasse</u> eats the lice off the backs of the salmon.

7) The fish can be <u>selectively bred</u> (see previous page) to produce <u>less aggressive</u>, <u>faster-growing</u> fish.

Paper 2

Fish Can Be Farmed in Tanks Too

Freshwater fish, e.g. <u>carp</u>, can be farmed in <u>ponds</u> or <u>indoors</u> in tanks where conditions can be <u>controlled</u>.
This is especially useful for controlling the <u>water quality</u>.

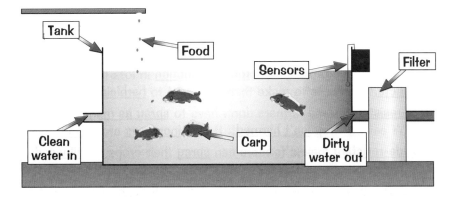

1) The <u>water</u> can be <u>monitored</u> to check that the <u>temperature</u>, <u>pH</u> and <u>oxygen level</u> is OK.

2) It's easy to control <u>how much food</u> is supplied and give <u>exactly the right sort</u> of food.

3) The water can be <u>removed</u> and <u>filtered</u> to get rid of <u>waste food</u> and <u>fish poo</u>.
This keeps the water <u>clean</u> for the fish and avoids <u>pollution</u> wherever the water ends up.

Two fish in a tank — one asks the other, "How do you drive this thing?"...

If you're thinking to yourself, "Why do we bother with all this faff? They're only fish." — think again. Fish are
an excellent source of protein — which we all need to grow up big and strong. They're also pretty darn tasty.

Q1   Explain one way that the diet supplied to the fish on a fish farm can improve the farm's output.   [2 marks]

Genetic Engineering

The basic idea of genetic engineering is to move <u>useful genes</u> from one organism's chromosomes into the cells of another. Although that sounds difficult, people have found <u>enzymes</u> and <u>vectors</u> (carriers) that can do it.

Enzymes Can Be Used To Cut Up DNA or Join DNA Pieces Together

1) <u>Restriction enzymes</u> recognise <u>specific sequences</u> of DNA and <u>cut the DNA</u> at these points.
2) <u>Ligase</u> enzymes are used to join <u>two pieces of DNA</u> together.
3) <u>Two different bits</u> of DNA stuck together are known as <u>recombinant DNA</u>.

Vectors Can Be Used To Insert DNA Into Other Organisms

A <u>vector</u> is something that's used to <u>transfer DNA</u> into a <u>cell</u>. There are two sorts — <u>plasmids</u> and <u>viruses</u>:

- Plasmids are <u>small</u>, <u>circular</u> molecules of DNA that can be <u>transferred</u> between <u>bacteria</u>.
- Viruses <u>insert</u> DNA into the organisms they <u>infect</u>.

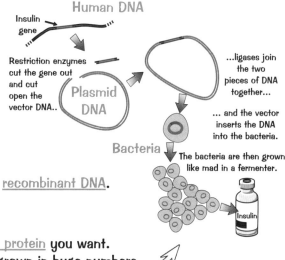

Here's how genetic engineering works:

1) The <u>DNA</u> you want to <u>insert</u> (e.g. the gene for human insulin) is cut out with a <u>restriction enzyme</u>. The <u>vector DNA</u> is then cut open using the <u>same</u> restriction enzyme.
2) The vector DNA and the DNA you're inserting are <u>mixed together</u> with <u>ligase enzymes</u>.
3) The ligases <u>join</u> the two pieces of DNA together to produce <u>recombinant DNA</u>.
4) The recombinant DNA (i.e. the vector containing new DNA) is <u>inserted</u> into other cells, e.g. bacteria.
5) These cells can now <u>use the gene you inserted</u> to <u>make the protein</u> you want. E.g. <u>bacteria</u> containing the gene for <u>human insulin</u> can be grown in huge numbers in a fermenter (see page 82) to produce <u>insulin</u> for people with <u>diabetes</u>.
6) Bacteria that contain the gene for human insulin are <u>transgenic</u> — this means that they contain <u>genes transferred from another species</u>. You can get transgenic animals and plants too.

Genetically Modified Plants Can Improve Food Production

1) Crops can be <u>genetically modified</u> to increase <u>food production</u> in lots of different ways — one is to make them <u>resistant to insects</u>, another is to make them resistant to <u>herbicides</u> (chemicals that kill plants).
2) Making crops <u>insect-resistant</u> means farmers don't have to <u>spray as many pesticides</u> (see page 81) — so <u>wildlife</u> that doesn't eat the crop <u>isn't harmed</u>. It also <u>increases</u> crop <u>yield</u>, making more <u>food</u>.
3) Making crops <u>herbicide-resistant</u> means farmers can <u>spray</u> their crops to <u>kill weeds</u>, <u>without affecting</u> the <u>crop</u> itself. This can also increase crop yield.
4) There are concerns about growing genetically modified crops though. One is that <u>transplanted genes</u> may get out into the <u>environment</u>. For example, a herbicide resistance gene may be picked up by weeds, creating a new 'superweed' variety. Another concern is that genetically modified crops could adversely affect <u>food chains</u> — or even <u>human health</u>.
5) Some people are against <u>genetic engineering</u> altogether — they <u>worry</u> that changing an organism's genes might create unforeseen <u>problems</u> — which could then get passed on to <u>future generations</u>.

If only there was a gene to make revision easier...

As genetic engineering advances, more questions will pop up about its implications. So it's a good idea to know both the benefits of genetic engineering and the problems presented by it — especially for the exam.

Q1   Explain one benefit of being able to genetically engineer herbicide-resistant crops.   [2 marks]

Cloning

Clones are <u>genetically identical organisms</u>. They can be made <u>artificially</u>, which is <u>great</u> if you have just one organism with really <u>useful properties</u> — cloning it gives you <u>lots more</u>.

Micropropagation is Used to Clone Plants

Plants can be cloned from existing plants using a technique called <u>micropropagation</u> (tissue culture):

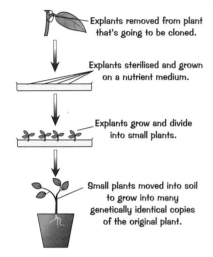

- Explants removed from plant that's going to be cloned.
- Explants sterilised and grown on a nutrient medium.
- Explants grow and divide into small plants.
- Small plants moved into soil to grow into many genetically identical copies of the original plant.

1) A plant with <u>desirable characteristics</u> (e.g. large fruit or pretty flowers) is selected to be <u>cloned</u>. Small pieces (called <u>explants</u>) are taken from the <u>tips of the stems</u> and the <u>side shoots</u> of this plant.

2) The explants are <u>sterilised</u> to kill any <u>microorganisms</u>.

3) The explants are then grown *in vitro* — they're placed in a <u>petri dish</u> containing a <u>nutrient medium</u>. The medium has all the nutrients the explants need to grow. It also contains <u>growth hormones</u>.

4) Cells in the explants <u>divide</u> and <u>grow</u> into a <u>small plant</u>. If <u>large quantities</u> of plants are required (e.g. to sell), further explants can be taken from these small plants, and so on until <u>enough</u> small plants are produced.

5) The <u>small plants</u> are taken out of the medium, <u>planted in soil</u> and put into <u>glasshouses</u> — they'll develop into plants that are <u>genetically identical</u> to the <u>original plant</u> — so they share the <u>same characteristics</u>.

Cloning an Adult Mammal is Done by Transplanting a Cell Nucleus

The <u>first mammal</u> to be successfully cloned from a <u>mature (adult) cell</u> was a sheep called "Dolly" in 1996. This is the method that was used to produce Dolly:

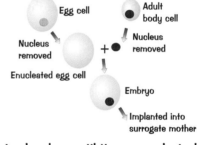

1) The <u>nucleus</u> of a sheep's <u>egg cell</u> was removed, creating an <u>enucleated cell</u> (i.e. a cell without a nucleus).

2) A <u>diploid</u> nucleus (with a full set of paired chromosomes — see page 53) was <u>inserted</u> in its place. This was a nucleus from a mature udder cell of a <u>different sheep</u>.

3) The cell was <u>stimulated</u> (by an electric shock) so that it started <u>dividing by mitosis</u>, as if it was a normal <u>fertilised egg</u>.

4) The dividing cell was <u>implanted</u> into the <u>uterus</u> of another sheep to develop until it was ready to be born.

5) The result was <u>Dolly</u>, a <u>clone</u> of the sheep that the <u>udder cell</u> came from.

<u>Other animals</u> can also be cloned using this method.

Cloned Transgenic Animals Can Be Used to Produce Human Proteins

1) <u>Cows</u> and <u>sheep</u> make <u>protein</u> naturally in their milk. By transferring human genes into the cells of these animals, researchers have managed to get them to produce useful <u>human proteins</u> in their milk.

Look back to the previous page for a reminder of what 'transgenic' means.

2) For example, they can produce <u>human antibodies</u> that can be used in therapy for illnesses like <u>arthritis</u>, some types of <u>cancer</u> and <u>multiple sclerosis</u>.

3) Transgenic <u>chickens</u> have also been engineered to produce human proteins in <u>egg white</u>.

4) These transgenic animals can then be <u>cloned</u> so that the useful genetic characteristic is <u>passed on</u> — this doesn't always happen with <u>breeding</u>.

Now try and transplant all this into your head...

Remember that genetic engineering and cloning are two different things, though transgenic animals can also be cloned.

Q1 A farmer discovers an apple tree in his orchard that has a very sweet-tasting fruit. Describe a method he could use to make clones of this tree. [4 marks]

Revision Questions for Section 9

And that's the final section finished. Award yourself a gold star and take a look at these beautiful questions.

- Try these questions and <u>tick off each one</u> when you <u>get it right</u>.
- When you've done <u>all the questions</u> for a topic and are <u>completely happy</u> with it, tick off the topic.

Increasing Crop Yields (p.81) ☐

1) How can farmers create the ideal conditions for photosynthesis inside a glasshouse? ☐
2) Why do farmers use fertilisers? ☐
3) Describe how biological control reduces pest numbers. ☐
4) Give one advantage and one disadvantage of using biological control instead of pesticides. ☐

Bacteria, Yoghurt, Yeast and Bread (p.82-83) ☐

5) Describe the process of making yoghurt. Don't forget to name the bacteria involved. ☐
6) List the conditions that have to be controlled in a fermenter. ☐
7) Describe how yeast is used to make bread rise. ☐
8) Describe an experiment to measure carbon dioxide production by yeast during anaerobic respiration. ☐

Selective Breeding (p.84) ☐

9) What is selective breeding? ☐
10) Give three examples of the use of selective breeding. ☐

Fish Farming (p.85) ☐

11) Describe how fish farms reduce the following:
   a) interspecific predation,
   b) intraspecific predation,
   c) disease. ☐
12) How can the water quality in fish farms be controlled? ☐

Genetic Engineering and Cloning (p.86-87) ☐

13) Describe the function of:
   a) a restriction enzyme,
   b) a ligase. ☐
14) What is a vector? ☐
15) Outline the important stages of genetically engineering a bacterium
to produce the human insulin gene. ☐
16) What is a transgenic organism? ☐
17) Describe one way plants can be genetically modified to help improve food production. ☐
18) Give an advantage of producing cloned plants. ☐
19) Describe the process of cloning an animal from a mature cell (e.g. cloning a sheep). ☐
20) Describe how cloned transgenic animals can be used to produce human proteins. ☐

Experimental Know-How

Pro scientists need to know how to plan and carry out scientific experiments. They also need to know how to interpret and evaluate the data they get from those experiments. Unluckily for you, those pesky examiners think you should be able to do the same — don't worry though, that's what this topic's all about.

You Might Get Asked Questions on Reliability and Validity

1) RELIABLE results come from experiments that give the same data:

- each time the experiment is repeated (by you),
- each time the experiment is reproduced by other scientists.

2) VALID results are both reliable AND come from experiments that were designed to be a fair test.

In the exam, you could be asked to suggest ways to improve the reliability or validity of some experimental results. If so, there are a couple of things to think about:

Controlling Variables Improves Validity

1) A variable is something that has the potential to change, e.g. temperature.
    In a lab experiment you usually change one variable and measure how it affects another variable.

> Example: you might change only the temperature of an enzyme-controlled reaction and measure how it affects the rate of reaction.

2) To make it a fair test, everything else that could affect the results should stay the same
    — otherwise you can't tell if the thing you're changing is causing the results or not.

> Example continued: you need to keep the pH the same, otherwise you won't know if any change in the rate of reaction is caused by the change in temperature, or the change in pH.

3) The variable you CHANGE is called the INDEPENDENT variable.
4) The variable you MEASURE is called the DEPENDENT variable.
5) The variables that you KEEP THE SAME are called CONTROL variables.

> Example continued:
> Independent variable = temperature
> Dependent variable = rate of reaction
> Control variables = pH, volume of reactants, concentration of reactants, etc.

6) Because you can't always control all the variables, you often need to use a CONTROL EXPERIMENT — an experiment that's kept under the same conditions as the rest of the investigation, but doesn't have anything done to it. This is so that you can see what happens when you don't change anything at all.

Carrying Out Repeats Improves Reliability

1) To improve reliability you need to repeat any measurements you make and calculate the mean (average).
2) You need to repeat each measurement at least three times.

Reliable results — they won't ever forget your birthday...

A typical exam question might describe an experiment, then ask you to suggest what variables need to be controlled. Don't panic, just use your scientific knowledge and a bit of common sense, e.g. if the experiment involves enzymes, you know that they're affected by things like temperature and pH, so these variables need to be kept constant (providing you're not actually measuring one of them). You might also need to say how you'd control the variables, e.g. the temperature of a reaction could be controlled using a water bath.

More Experimental Know-How

Thought you knew <u>everything</u> there was to know about experiments? <u>Think again</u> my friend...

You Might Have to Suggest Ways to Make an Experiment Safer

1) It's important that experiments are safe. If you're asked to suggest ways to make an experiment safer, you'll first need to identify what the <u>potential hazards</u> might be. Hazards include things like:

> - <u>Microorganisms</u>, e.g. some bacteria can make you ill.
> - <u>Chemicals</u>, e.g. hydrochloric acid can burn your skin and alcohols catch fire easily.
> - <u>Fire</u>, e.g. an unattended Bunsen burner is a fire hazard.
> - <u>Electricity</u>, e.g. faulty electrical equipment could give you a shock.

Hmm... Where did my acid go?

2) Then you'll need to suggest ways of <u>reducing</u> the <u>risks</u> involved with the hazard, e.g.

> - If you're working with <u>hydrochloric acid</u>, always wear gloves and safety goggles. This will reduce the risk of the acid coming into contact with your skin and eyes.
> - If you're using a <u>Bunsen burner</u>, stand it on a heat proof mat. This will reduce the risk of starting a fire.

You can find out about potential hazards by looking in textbooks, doing some internet research, or asking your teacher.

You Could be Asked About Accuracy...

1) It's important that results are <u>accurate</u>. Accurate results are those that are <u>really close</u> to the <u>true answer</u>.

2) The accuracy of your results usually depends on your <u>method</u>.

> E.g. say you wanted to measure the <u>rate</u> of an <u>enzyme-controlled reaction</u> that releases a <u>gas</u> as a product. The rate of the reaction would be the <u>amount of gas produced per unit time</u>. You could <u>estimate</u> how much gas is produced by <u>counting</u> the number of <u>bubbles</u> that are released. But the bubbles could be <u>different sizes</u>, and if they're produced really quickly you might <u>miss some</u> when counting. It would be more accurate to <u>collect the gas</u> (e.g. in a gas cylinder) and <u>measure</u> its <u>volume</u>.

3) To make sure your results are as <u>accurate</u> as possible, you need to make sure you're measuring the <u>right thing</u> and that you <u>don't miss</u> anything or <u>include</u> anything that shouldn't be included in the measurements.

> E.g. if you want to know the <u>length</u> of a <u>potato chip</u>, you need to <u>start measuring</u> from '<u>0 cm</u>' on the ruler, <u>not</u> the <u>very end</u> of the ruler (or your measurement will be a few mm too short).

...And Precision

Results also need to be <u>precise</u>. Precise results are the ones where the data is <u>all really close</u> to the <u>mean</u> (average) of your repeated results (i.e. not spread out).

Sometimes, results are described as precise if they've been taken using sensitive instruments that can measure in small increments, e.g. using a ruler with a millimetre scale gives more precise data than a ruler with a scale in centimetres.

Repeat	Data set 1	Data set 2
1	12	11
2	14	17
3	13	14
Mean	13	14

Data set 1 is more precise than data set 2.

Not revising — an unacceptable exam hazard...

It may interest you to know that you won't just have to write about other people's experiments in the exam. Sometimes you'll be asked to describe how you'd carry out your own experiment and all this stuff about reliability and what not will apply then too. Ah. From the look on your face, I'm guessing it didn't interest you to know that.

Sampling and Ethics

I love samples... especially when I'm a bit peckish in the supermarket and they're handing out free cheese. Unfortunately, this page isn't about those samples. It's a lot more useful than that...

Sampling Should be Random

1) When you're investigating a population, it's generally not possible to study every single organism in the population. This means that you need to take samples of the population you're interested in.

2) The sample data will be used to draw conclusions about the whole population, so it's important that it accurately represents the whole population.

3) To make sure a sample represents the population, it should be random.

If a sample doesn't represent the population as a whole, it's said to be biased.

Organisms Should Be Sampled At Random Sites in an Area

1) If you're interested in the distribution of an organism in an area, or its population size, you can take population samples in the area you're interested in using quadrats or transects (see page 72).

2) If you only take samples from one part of the area, your results will be biased — they may not give an accurate representation of the whole area.

3) To make sure that your sampling isn't biased, you need to use a method of choosing sampling sites in which every site has an equal chance of being chosen. For example:

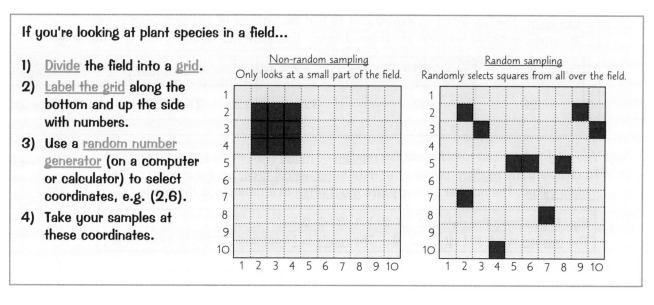

If you're looking at plant species in a field...

1) Divide the field into a grid.
2) Label the grid along the bottom and up the side with numbers.
3) Use a random number generator (on a computer or calculator) to select coordinates, e.g. (2,6).
4) Take your samples at these coordinates.

Non-random sampling — Only looks at a small part of the field.
Random sampling — Randomly selects squares from all over the field.

You Need to Think About Ethical Issues In Your Experiments

1) Any organisms involved in your investigations need to be treated safely and ethically.

2) Animals need to be treated humanely — they should be handled carefully and any wild animals captured for studying (e.g. during an investigation of the distribution of an organism) should be returned to their original habitat.

3) Any animals kept in the lab should also be cared for in a humane way, e.g. they should not be kept in overcrowded conditions.

4) If you are carrying out an experiment involving other students (e.g. investigating the effect of exercise on breathing rate), they should not be forced to participate against their will or feel pressured to take part.

'Eeny, meeny, miny, moe' just doesn't cut it any more...

Sampling is a vital part of an investigation. It needs to be done randomly, or the data won't be worth much. Also, just before you go wandering off, remember — you've got to be kind and caring to all of those critters (and fellow students...) that you might be using in your investigations. Ethics are really important in science.

Drawing Graphs and Interpreting Results

If you're presented with some results from an experiment you've got to know <u>what to do with them</u>.

You Should Be Able to Identify Anomalous Results

1) Most results vary a bit, but any that are <u>totally different</u> are called <u>anomalous results</u>.

2) They're <u>caused</u> by <u>human errors</u>, e.g. by a mistake made when measuring or by not setting up a piece of equipment properly.

3) You could be asked to <u>identify</u> an anomalous result in the exam and suggest what <u>caused</u> it — just look for a result that <u>doesn't fit in</u> with the rest (e.g. it's <u>too high</u> or <u>too low</u>) then try to figure out what could have <u>gone wrong</u> with the experiment to have caused it.

4) If you're calculating an <u>average</u>, you can <u>ignore</u> any anomalous results.

You Might Have to Process Your Data

1) When you've done repeats of an experiment you should always calculate the <u>mean</u> (a type of average). To do this <u>add together</u> all the data values and <u>divide</u> by the total number of values in the sample.

2) You might also need to calculate the <u>range</u> (how spread out the data is). To do this find the <u>largest</u> number and <u>subtract</u> the <u>smallest</u> number from it.

Ignore anomalous results when calculating these.

> <u>Example</u>: The results of an experiment to find the volume of gas produced in an enzyme-controlled reaction are shown below. Calculate the mean volume and the range.
>
> | Repeat 1 (cm³) | Repeat 2 (cm³) | Repeat 3 (cm³) | Mean (cm³) | Range (cm³) |
> |---|---|---|---|---|
> | 28 | 37 | 32 | (28 + 37 + 32) ÷ 3 = 32 | 37 − 28 = 9 |

3) You might also need to calculate the <u>median</u> or <u>mode</u> (two more types of average). To calculate the <u>median</u>, put all your data in <u>numerical order</u> — the median is the <u>middle value</u>. The number that appears <u>most often</u> in a data set is the <u>mode</u>.

If you have an even number of values, the median is halfway between the middle two values.

> E.g. If you have the data set: 1 2 1 1 3 4 2
> The <u>median</u> is: 1 1 1 <u>2</u> 2 3 4. The <u>mode</u> is <u>1</u> because 1 appears most often.

Bar Charts can be Used to Show Different Types of Data

<u>Bar charts</u> are used to display:

1) <u>Categoric data</u> — data that comes in <u>distinct categories</u>, e.g. flower colour, blood group.

2) <u>Discrete data</u> — data that can be counted in <u>chunks</u>, where there's no in-between value, e.g. number of bacteria is discrete because you can't have half a bacterium.

3) <u>Continuous data</u> — <u>numerical</u> data that can have any <u>value</u> in a <u>range</u>, e.g. length, volume, temperature.

There are some <u>golden rules</u> you need to follow for <u>drawing</u> bar charts:

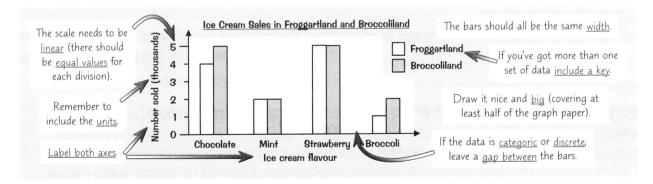

The scale needs to be <u>linear</u> (there should be <u>equal values</u> for each division).

Remember to include the <u>units</u>.

<u>Label both axes</u>.

The bars should all be the same <u>width</u>.

If you've got more than one set of data <u>include a key</u>.

Draw it nice and <u>big</u> (covering at least half of the graph paper).

If the data is <u>categoric</u> or <u>discrete</u>, leave a <u>gap between</u> the bars.

Drawing Graphs and Interpreting Results

Graphs can be Used to Plot Continuous Data

If both variables are <u>continuous</u> you should use a <u>graph</u> to display the data.

Here are the rules for plotting points on a graph:

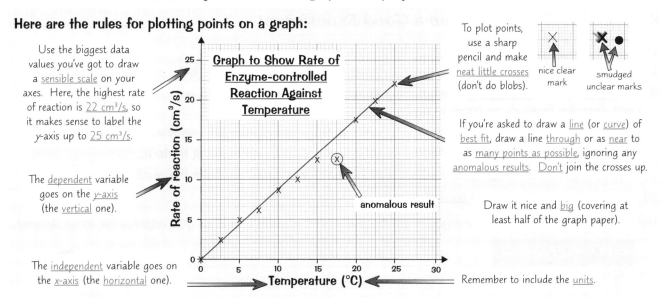

Use the biggest data values you've got to draw a <u>sensible scale</u> on your axes. Here, the highest rate of reaction is <u>22 cm³/s</u>, so it makes sense to label the y-axis up to <u>25 cm³/s</u>.

The <u>dependent</u> variable goes on the <u>y-axis</u> (the <u>vertical</u> one).

The <u>independent</u> variable goes on the <u>x-axis</u> (the <u>horizontal</u> one).

To plot points, use a sharp pencil and make <u>neat little crosses</u> (don't do blobs). nice clear mark / smudged unclear marks

If you're asked to draw a <u>line</u> (or <u>curve</u>) of <u>best fit</u>, draw a line <u>through</u> or as <u>near</u> to as <u>many points as possible</u>, ignoring any <u>anomalous results</u>. <u>Don't</u> join the crosses up.

Draw it nice and <u>big</u> (covering at least half of the graph paper).

Remember to include the <u>units</u>.

You Need to be Able to Interpret Graphs

1) A graph is used to show the <u>relationship</u> between two variables — you need to be able to look at a graph and <u>describe</u> this relationship.

> <u>Example:</u> The graph above shows that as <u>temperature increases, so does rate of reaction.</u>

A relationship is directly proportional if one variable increases at the same rate as the other variable. E.g. if one variable doubles, the other also doubles. This is only true if the line is straight and goes through the origin (O,O).

2) You also need to be able to <u>read information</u> off a graph. In this example, to find what the rate of reaction was at <u>11 °C</u>, you'd draw a <u>vertical line up</u> to the graph line from the x-axis at 11 °C and a <u>horizontal line across</u> to the y-axis. This would tell you that the rate of reaction at 11 °C was around <u>9.7 cm³/s</u>.

Graphs Show the Correlation Between Two Variables

1) You can get <u>three</u> types of <u>correlation</u> (relationship) between variables:

2) Just because there's correlation, it doesn't mean the change in one variable is <u>causing</u> the change in the other — there might be <u>other factors</u> involved.

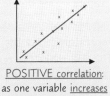 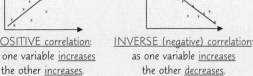 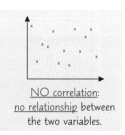

<u>POSITIVE</u> correlation: as one variable <u>increases</u> the other <u>increases</u>.

<u>INVERSE</u> (negative) correlation: as one variable <u>increases</u> the other <u>decreases</u>.

<u>NO</u> correlation: <u>no relationship</u> between the two variables.

3) There are three possible reasons for a correlation:

- <u>CHANCE:</u> It might seem strange, but two things can show a correlation purely due to <u>chance</u>.
- <u>LINKED BY A 3RD VARIABLE:</u> A lot of the time it may <u>look</u> as if a change in one variable is causing a change in the other, but it <u>isn't</u> — a <u>third variable links</u> the two things.
- <u>CAUSE:</u> Sometimes a change in one variable does <u>cause</u> a change in the other. You can only conclude that a correlation is due to cause when you've <u>controlled all the variables</u> that could, just could, be affecting the result.

I love eating apples — I call it core elation...

Science is all about finding relationships between things. And I don't mean that scientists gather together in corners to discuss whether or not Devini and Sebastian might be a couple... though they probably do that too.

Planning Experiments

In the exam, you could be asked to <u>plan</u> or <u>describe</u> how you'd <u>carry out</u> an experiment. The experiment might be one you've already come across (easy) or (gasp) you might be asked to come up with an <u>experiment of your own</u> to test something. I know. Examiners are <u>harsh</u>. It's not as bad as it sounds though.

You Need to Be Able to Plan a Good Experiment

Here are some <u>general tips</u> on what to include when planning an experiment:

1) Say <u>what</u> you're <u>measuring</u> (i.e. what the <u>dependent variable</u> is going to be).
2) Say <u>what</u> you're <u>changing</u> (i.e. what the <u>independent variable</u> is going to be) and describe <u>how</u> you're going to change it.
3) Describe the <u>method</u> and the <u>apparatus</u> you'd use (e.g. to measure the variables).
4) Describe what <u>variables</u> you're keeping <u>constant</u> — and <u>how</u> you're going to do it.
5) Say that you need to <u>repeat</u> the experiment at least three times, to make the results <u>more reliable</u>.
6) Say whether you're using a <u>control</u> or not.

> Even if you can't remember all the details of an experimental method you've learned about, you could still get marks for describing things like the independent and dependent variables.

Here's an <u>idea</u> of the sort of thing you might be asked in the exam and what you might write as an answer...

Exam-style Question:

1 Describe an investigation to find out what effect temperature has on the rate of photosynthesis in Canadian pondweed.   (6 marks)

Example Answer:

Set up a test tube containing a measured amount of Canadian pondweed, water and sodium hydrogencarbonate. Connect the test tube up to a capillary tube containing water and a syringe, then place it in a water bath in front of a source of white light.

Leave the pondweed to photosynthesise for a set amount of time. As it photosynthesises, the oxygen released will collect in the capillary tube. At the end of the experiment, use the syringe to draw the gas bubble in the tube up alongside a ruler and measure the length of the gas bubble. This is proportional to the volume of O_2 produced.

Repeat the experiment with the water bath set to different temperatures (e.g. 10 °C, 20 °C, 30 °C and 40 °C).

The pondweed should be left to photosynthesise for the same amount of time at each temperature (monitored using a stopwatch). The test tubes should also be set up the same distance away from the light source (measured using a ruler) and the same mass of pondweed should be used in each test tube (measured using a balance).

A control should also be set up at each temperature. This should be a test tube containing water and boiled pondweed (so that it can't photosynthesise).

Repeat the experiment three times at each temperature. Use the results to find an average rate of photosynthesis at each temperature. This will make the results more reliable.

Experiments Test Hypotheses

1) A <u>hypothesis</u> is a possible <u>explanation</u> for something that you've observed.
2) You can use experiments to <u>test</u> whether a hypothesis might be <u>right or not</u>. This involves making a <u>prediction</u> based on the hypothesis and testing it by <u>gathering evidence</u> (i.e. <u>data</u>) from <u>investigations</u>. If <u>evidence</u> from <u>experiments</u> backs up a prediction, you're a step closer to figuring out if the hypothesis is true.

> I'm thinking of throwing a surprise party for Saturn.

> Make sure you planet first...

Plan your way to exam success...

The number of marks available for a question like this will vary, but it'll usually be around five or six. This means you'll have to write an extended answer. Think about what you're going to say beforehand and in what order — that way you're less likely to forget something important. Like what it is you're actually measuring, say.

Describing Experiments

Conclusions and Evaluations

Congratulations — you're nearly at the end of a gruelling investigation, time to draw conclusions and evaluate.

You Can Only Conclude What the Data Shows and NO MORE

1) Drawing conclusions might seem pretty straightforward — you just look at your data and say what pattern or relationship you see between the dependent and independent variables.

The table on the right shows the heights of pea plant seedlings grown for three weeks with different fertilisers.

Fertiliser	Mean growth / mm
A	13.5
B	19.5
No fertiliser	5.5

CONCLUSION:
Fertiliser B makes pea plant seedlings grow taller over a three week period than fertiliser A.

2) But you've got to be really careful that your conclusion matches the data you've got and doesn't go any further.

You can't conclude that fertiliser B makes any other type of plant grow taller than fertiliser A — the results could be totally different.

3) You also need to be able to use your results to justify your conclusion (i.e. back up your conclusion with some specific data).

Over the three week period, fertiliser B made the pea plants grow 6 mm more on average than fertiliser A.

4) When writing a conclusion you need to refer back to the original hypothesis and say whether the data supports it or not:

The hypothesis for this experiment might have been that adding fertiliser would increase the growth of plants because it would provide plants with nutrients. The prediction may have been that fertiliser B contained more nutrients and so would increase growth more than fertiliser A. If so, the data increases confidence in the hypothesis.

Evaluations — Describe How it Could be Improved

An evaluation is a critical analysis of the whole investigation.

1) You should comment on the method — was it valid? Did you control all the other variables to make it a fair test?

2) Comment on the quality of the results — was there enough evidence to reach a valid conclusion? Were the results reliable, valid, accurate and precise?

3) Were there any anomalous results? If there were none then say so. If there were any, try to explain them — were they caused by errors in measurement? Were there any other variables that could have affected the results?

4) All this analysis will allow you to say how confident you are that your conclusion is right.

5) Then you can suggest any changes to the method that would improve the quality of the results, so that you could have more confidence in your conclusion. For example, you might suggest changing the way you controlled a variable, or increasing the number of measurements you took. Taking more measurements at narrower intervals could give you a more accurate result. For example:

Enzymes have an optimum temperature (a temperature at which they work best). Say you do an experiment to find an enzyme's optimum temperature and take measurements at 10 °C, 20 °C, 30 °C, 40 °C and 50 °C. The results of this experiment tell you the optimum is 40 °C. You could then repeat the experiment, taking more measurements around 40 °C to get a more accurate value for the optimum.

6) You could also make more predictions based on your conclusion, then further experiments could be carried out to test them.

When suggesting improvements to the investigation, always make sure that you say why you think this would make the results better.

Evaluation — next time, I'll make sure I don't burn the lab down...

And that's a wrap. Well, not quite. You've still got the small matter of the whole exam shenanigans to look forward to. Around 20% of your marks will come from being able to describe experiments, and analysing and evaluating data and methods in an appropriate way. So, make sure you're happy with everything in this section. Best of luck.

Describing Experiments

Answers

Section 1 — The Nature and Variety of Organisms

Page 1 — Characteristics of Living Organisms
Q1 excretion *[1 mark]*

Page 2 — Levels of Organisation
Q1 Any two from: e.g. plant cells have chloroplasts but animal cells don't. / Plant cells have a cell wall, but animal cells don't. / Plant cells have a vacuole, but animal cells don't. *[2 marks]*

Page 3 — Specialised Cells and Stem Cells
Q1 E.g. red blood cell / white blood cell *[1 mark]*.
Q2 Advantage: e.g. stem cells can be transferred from the bone marrow of a healthy person to replace faulty blood cells in the patient who receives them. / Embryonic stem cells could be used to replace faulty cells in sick people/make insulin-producing cells for people with diabetes/ make nerve cells for people paralysed by spinal injuries *[1 mark]*.
Disadvantage: e.g. stem cells grown in the lab may become contaminated with a virus which could be passed on to the patient and so make them sicker *[1 mark]*.

Page 4 — Plants, Animals and Fungi
Q1 As sucrose *[1 mark]* and as starch *[1 mark]*.
Q2 E.g. yeast *[1 mark]*

Page 5 — Protctists, Bacteria and Viruses
Q1 E.g. tobacco mosaic virus *[1 mark]*

Page 6 — Enzymes
Q1 If the pH is too high or too low, the pH interferes with the bonds holding the enzyme together. This changes the shape of the active site *[1 mark]* and denatures the enzyme *[1 mark]*.

Page 7 — Investigating Enzyme Activity
Q1 Any two from: e.g. the pH of the reaction mixture / the volume of hydrogen peroxide used / the concentration of hydrogen peroxide used / the type of potato used / the size of the potato cube used *[2 marks]*.

Page 8 — Diffusion
Q1 The ink will diffuse/spread out through the water *[1 mark]*. This is because the ink particles will move from where there is a higher concentration of them (the drop of ink) to where there is a lower concentration of them (the surrounding water) *[1 mark]*.

Page 9 — Osmosis
Q1 Osmosis is the net movement of water molecules across a partially permeable membrane *[1 mark]* from a region of higher water concentration to a region of lower water concentration *[1 mark]*. / Osmosis is the net movement of water molecules across a partially permeable membrane *[1 mark]* from a region of lower solute concentration to a region of higher solute concentration *[1 mark]*.
Q2 If the cell is short of water, the solution inside it will be quite concentrated. The solution outside of the cell will be more dilute *[1 mark]*, and so water will move into the cell by osmosis *[1 mark]*.

Page 10 — Diffusion and Osmosis Experiments
Q1 Water will move out of the piece of potato by osmosis *[1 mark]*, so its mass will decrease *[1 mark]*.

Page 11 — Active Transport
Q1 surface area = 5 × 5 × 6 = 150 cm²
volume = 5 × 5 × 5 = 125 cm³
surface area : volume ratio
= 150 : 125
= 6 : 5 *[1 mark]*

Section 2 — Human Nutrition

Page 13 — Biological Molecules and Food Tests
Q1 carbohydrate *[1 mark]*
Q2 carbon, nitrogen, hydrogen and oxygen *[1 mark]*
Q3 Break up the food using a pestle and mortar *[1 mark]*. Transfer the ground up food to a beaker and add some distilled water *[1 mark]*. Give the mixture a stir with a glass rod to dissolve some of the food *[1 mark]*. Filter the solution using a funnel lined with filter paper to get rid of the solid bits of food *[1 mark]*.

Page 14 — Food Tests
Q1 E.g. biuret solution *[1 mark]*

Page 15 — A Balanced Diet
Q1 E.g. liver *[1 mark]*
Q2 Iron is needed to make haemoglobin for healthy blood *[1 mark]*.

Page 16 — Energy From Food
Q1 energy in food = mass of water × temperature change of water × 4.2
= 30 × 18 × 4.2
= **2268 J** *[1 mark]*

Page 17 — Enzymes and Digestion
Q1 peristalsis *[1 mark]*

Page 18 — The Alimentary Canal
Q1 E.g. duodenum *[1 mark]*, ileum *[1 mark]*

Section 3 — Plant Nutrition and Transport

Page 20 — Photosynthesis
Q1 glucose *[1 mark]*, oxygen *[1 mark]*

Page 21 — Rate of Photosynthesis
Q1 Initially, as the temperature increases, the rate of photosynthesis increases *[1 mark]*. However, if the temperature gets too high, the plant's enzymes will be denatured *[1 mark]*, so the rate of photosynthesis will rapidly decrease *[1 mark]*.

Page 22 — Photosynthesis Experiments
Q1 iodine *[1 mark]*

Page 23 — More Photosynthesis Experiments
Q1 Plants produce glucose during photosynthesis. Some of this glucose is stored as starch *[1 mark]*. If you perform the starch test on a leaf grown without light, the leaf will not turn blue-black *[1 mark]*. This means that there is no starch present in the leaf *[1 mark]*. As no starch has been made in the leaf grown without light, it shows that light is needed for plants to photosynthesise *[1 mark]*.

Page 24 — Minerals for Healthy Growth
Q1 They are needed to make amino acids and proteins *[1 mark]*, which are needed for growth *[1 mark]*.
Q2 Plants use magnesium to make chlorophyll, which is needed for photosynthesis — so without magnesium, plants won't have the chlorophyll they need to photosynthesise *[1 mark]*.

Page 25 — Transport in Plants
Q1 phloem tubes *[1 mark]*

Page 26 — Transpiration
Q1 As it gets darker, the stomata begin to close *[1 mark]*. This means that very little water can escape *[1 mark]* and the rate of transpiration decreases *[1 mark]*.

Page 27 — Measuring Transpiration
Q1 Any two from: e.g. air humidity / light intensity / wind speed/air movement / size of plant *[2 marks]*

Section 4 — Respiration and Gas Exchange

Page 29 — Respiration
Q1 The leg muscles didn't get enough oxygen during the sprint, so began to use anaerobic respiration *[1 mark]*. This resulted in the production of lactic acid *[1 mark]*. The build up of lactic acid in the muscles caused cramp *[1 mark]*.

Page 30 — Investigating Respiration
Q1 E.g. soak some dried beans in water until they germinate *[1 mark]*. Boil the same amount of dried beans to kill them so they can't respire/to act as a control *[1 mark]*. Put the same amount of hydrogen-carbonate indicator into two test tubes *[1 mark]*. Place the germinating beans and dead beans on a gauze platform in the separate test tubes *[1 mark]*. Seal each test tube with a rubber bung and leave the apparatus for one hour *[1 mark]*. Observe and record any changes to the colour of the hydrogen-carbonate indicator *[1 mark]*.

Page 31 — Gas Exchange — Flowering Plants
Q1 Through the stomata *[1 mark]*.

Page 32 — Gas Exchange — Flowering Plants
Q1 The hydrogen-carbonate indicator will turn yellow *[1 mark]*. The foil blocks out all light, so respiration will still take place but there will be no photosynthesis *[1 mark]*. So the concentration of carbon dioxide in the test tube will increase *[1 mark]*.

Page 33 — The Respiratory System and Ventilation
Q1 The intercostal muscles and the diaphragm contract *[1 mark]*. This increases the volume of the thorax, which decreases the pressure and so draws air in *[1 mark]*. The intercostal muscles and the diaphragm then relax *[1 mark]*. This decreases the volume of the thorax, which forces air out *[1 mark]*.
Q2 Air goes through the nose and mouth to the trachea *[1 mark]*. It then passes through the bronchi *[1 mark]* and then through the bronchioles *[1 mark]* to the alveoli.

Page 34 — Investigating Breathing
Q1 E.g. the time spent exercising / the temperature of the room *[2 marks]*.
Q2 The air blown through the limewater by the student contains carbon dioxide (from respiration) which turns the limewater cloudy *[1 mark]*.

Page 35 — Gas Exchange — Humans
Q1 Any one from: e.g. they have a large surface area. / They have a moist lining for dissolving gases. / They have very thin walls. / They have a good blood supply. / The walls are permeable *[1 mark]*.

Answers

Section 5 — Blood and Organs

Page 37 — Functions of the Blood
Q1 Red blood cells are small and have a biconcave shape to give a large surface area for absorbing and releasing oxygen *[1 mark]*. They contain haemoglobin which can combine with oxygen in the lungs and release it in body tissues *[1 mark]*. Red blood cells don't have a nucleus — this frees up space for more haemoglobin, so they can carry more oxygen *[1 mark]*.

Page 38 — White Blood Cells and Immunity
Q1 Phagocytes engulf and digest pathogens *[1 mark]*.

Page 39 — Blood Vessels
Q1 They have a big lumen to help the blood flow despite the low pressure *[1 mark]* and they have valves to keep the blood flowing in the right direction *[1 mark]*.

Page 40 — The Heart
Q1 Adrenaline binds to specific receptors in the heart *[1 mark]*. This causes the cardiac muscle to contract more frequently *[1 mark]*, so heart rate increases *[1 mark]*.

Page 41 — Circulation and Coronary Heart Disease
Q1 renal vein *[1 mark]*

Page 42 — Excretion — The Kidneys
Q1 Any two from: urea / ions / water *[2 marks]*.

Page 43 — Osmoregulation — The Kidneys
Q1 Sweating *[1 mark]*, breathing *[1 mark]* and in urine *[1 mark]*.
Q2 ADH makes the collecting ducts of the kidney nephrons more permeable *[1 mark]* so more water is reabsorbed back into the blood *[1 mark]*.

Section 6 — Coordination and Response

Page 45 — The Nervous System and Responding to Stimuli
Q1 brain *[1 mark]*, spinal cord *[1 mark]*

Page 46 — Reflexes
Q1 Impulses are sent from receptors in his hand along a sensory neurone to the CNS *[1 mark]*. In the CNS, the sensory neurone passes on the message to a relay neurone *[1 mark]*. The relay neurone relays the impulse to a motor neurone *[1 mark]* and the impulse then travels along the motor neurone to the effector (a muscle in his arm) *[1 mark]*.

Page 47 — The Eye
Q1 The ciliary muscles contract *[1 mark]*, which slackens the suspensory ligaments *[1 mark]*. The lens becomes fat/more curved *[1 mark]*. This increases the amount by which it refracts light, so the image is focused on the retina *[1 mark]*.

Page 48 — Hormones
Q1 the ovaries *[1 mark]*

Page 49 — Homeostasis
Q1 The runner will lose water in sweat/through the breath *[1 mark]*, and so less water will be lost in urine *[1 mark]*.

Page 50 — More on Homeostasis
Q1 a) Less blood flows near the surface of the skin *[1 mark]* because vasoconstriction occurs in the blood vessels near the surface *[1 mark]*.
  b) Very little sweat is produced *[1 mark]*.

Page 51 — Responses in Plants
Q1 More auxin accumulates on the side of the shoot that's in the shade *[1 mark]*. This causes the cells on the shaded side of the shoot to elongate faster *[1 mark]* so the shoot bends towards the light.

Section 7 — Reproduction and Inheritance

Page 53 — DNA, Genes and Chromosomes
Q1 A gene is a short section of DNA *[1 mark]* that codes for a particular protein *[1 mark]*.

Page 54 — Protein Synthesis
Q1 The order of bases in a gene determines the order of amino acids in a protein *[1 mark]*. Each gene contains a different order of bases, which can code for a particular protein *[1 mark]*.
Q2 7 *[1 mark]*

Page 55 — More on Protein Synthesis
Q1 RNA polymerase binds to a region of non-coding DNA in front of the gene to be transcribed *[1 mark]*. The two strands of DNA unzip and the RNA polymerase moves along the coding DNA *[1 mark]*. As the RNA polymerase moves along, it joins together RNA molecules that are complementary to the base sequence of the coding DNA *[1 mark]*.

Page 56 — Asexual Reproduction and Mitosis
Q1 The DNA in the cell duplicates and forms X-shaped chromosomes *[1 mark]*. The chromosomes then line up at the centre of the cell *[1 mark]*. Cell fibres pull the chromosomes apart and the two arms of each chromosome go to opposite ends of the cell *[1 mark]*. Membranes form around each set of chromosomes forming the nuclei of the two new cells *[1 mark]*. The cytoplasm then divides forming two new cells *[1 mark]*.

Page 57 — Sexual Reproduction and Meiosis
Q1 When the cell divides, some of the chromosomes from the organism's father and some of the chromosomes from the organism's mother go into each new cell *[1 mark]*. The mixing up of the chromosomes/genes creates genetic variation *[1 mark]*.

Page 58 — Sexual Reproduction in Plants
Q1 Any two from: e.g. they have small, dull petals *[1 mark]* because they don't need to attract insects *[1 mark]*. / They don't have nectaries or strong scents *[1 mark]* because they don't need to attract insects *[1 mark]*. / They have a lot of small and light pollen grains *[1 mark]* which can easily be carried by the wind *[1 mark]*. / They have long filaments that hang the anthers outside the flower *[1 mark]* so that a lot of the pollen gets blown away by the wind *[1 mark]*. / They have a large feathery stigma *[1 mark]* to catch pollen as it's carried past by the wind *[1 mark]*.

Page 59 — Fertilisation and Germination in Plants
Q1 The seed uses glucose from a store of food reserves *[1 mark]* for respiration to transfer energy *[1 mark]*.

Page 60 — Investigating Seed Germination
Q1 a) No germination will have taken place *[1 mark]*.
  b) The temperature was too cold for germination to occur *[1 mark]*.

Page 61 — Asexual Reproduction in Plants
Q1 E.g. plants can be produced cheaply/quickly. / If you have a good parent plant, you can produce a genetically identical clone *[1 mark]*.

Page 62 — Human Reproductive Systems
Q1 Any three from: e.g. extra hair on underarms and pubic area / widening of hips / development of breasts / ovum release and start of periods *[3 marks]*.

Page 63 — The Menstrual Cycle and Pregnancy
Q1 The placenta lets the blood of the embryo and mother get very close to allow the exchange of food, oxygen and waste *[1 mark]*.

Page 64 — Genetic Diagrams
Q1 The genotype is the alleles that an individual has *[1 mark]*. The phenotype is the characteristics that an individual's alleles produce *[1 mark]*.

Page 65 — More Genetic Diagrams
Q1

	T	t
t	Tt	tt
t	Tt	tt

long tailed : short tailed
1 : 1
[1 mark for correct gametes, 1 mark for correct offspring genotypes and 1 mark for correct ratio.]

Page 66 — Family Pedigrees and Sex Determination
Q1 Ff and ff *[1 mark]*.

Page 67 — Variation
Q1 Any two from: e.g. sunlight / moisture level / temperature / mineral content of the soil *[2 marks]*.

Page 68 — Evolution and Natural Selection
Q1 Some of the musk oxen may have had a gene/allele which gave them thicker fur *[1 mark]*. These oxen would have been more likely to survive and reproduce *[1 mark]* and so pass on the gene/allele for thicker fur *[1 mark]*. This process of natural selection may have continued over many generations, until all of the musk oxen had thick fur *[1 mark]*.

Page 69 — Mutations and Antibiotic Resistance
Q1 A bacterium can develop a random mutation in its DNA *[1 mark]*, which may mean that it is less affected by a particular antibiotic *[1 mark]*. This means that it is better able to survive in a host who is being treated with that antibiotic *[1 mark]*, and so it lives for longer and is able to reproduce many more times *[1 mark]*. This leads to the allele for resistance being passed on to lots of offspring, and it becomes more common in the population over time *[1 mark]*.

Answers

Section 8 — Ecology and the Environment

Page 71 — Ecosystems and Biodiversity
Q1 Any two from: e.g. temperature / moisture level / light intensity / pH of the soil / toxic chemicals *[2 marks]*

Page 72 — Using Quadrats
Q1 $1 \div 0.25 = 4$
$0.75 \times 4 = 3$ buttercups per m² *[1 mark]*
$3 \times 1200 = 3600$ buttercups in total *[1 mark]*

Page 73 — Pyramids of Number, Biomass and Energy
Q1 The mass of living material at that stage of the food chain *[1 mark]*.

Page 74 — Energy Transfer and Food Webs
Q1 E.g. the population of grasshoppers could increase *[1 mark]* as there's nothing to eat them *[1 mark]*. The population of snakes could decrease *[1 mark]* as there's nothing for them to eat *[1 mark]*.

Page 75 — The Carbon Cycle
Q1 Any two from: e.g. not as much CO_2 in the air gets used for photosynthesis. / Microorganisms involved in the decomposition of the dead trees release CO_2 into the atmosphere through respiration. / Burning chopped down trees releases CO_2 into the air *[2 marks]*.

Page 76 — The Nitrogen Cycle
Q1 It makes nitrogen react with oxygen in the air to give nitrates *[1 mark]*.
Q2 Decomposers turn proteins in dead leaves into ammonia, which goes on to form ammonium ions in the soil *[1 mark]*. Then nitrifying bacteria turn the ammonium ions into nitrates *[1 mark]*.

Page 77 — Air Pollution
Q1 Sulfur dioxide mixes with clouds to form dilute sulfuric acid *[1 mark]*. This then falls as acid rain *[1 mark]*. Acid rain can result in the death of plants and animals *[1 mark]*.

Page 78 — The Greenhouse Effect
Q1 Any three from: e.g. carbon dioxide / methane / CFCs / nitrous oxide / water vapour *[3 marks]*

Page 79 — Water Pollution and Deforestation
Q1 E.g. applying too much fertiliser to fields / pollution of water by sewage *[1 mark]*.

Section 9 — Use of Biological Resources

Page 81 — Increasing Crop Yields
Q1 Increasing the temperature and carbon dioxide concentration increases the rate of photosynthesis *[1 mark]*. This means that the plants grow bigger and faster and so crop yields are increased *[1 mark]*.

Page 82 — Bacteria and Making Yoghurt
Q1 The paddles circulate (or agitate) the medium around the vessel *[1 mark]*. This ensures that the microorganisms can always access the nutrients needed for growth, increasing the product yield *[1 mark]*.

Page 83 — Yeast and Making Bread
Q1 The high temperatures in the oven kill the yeast *[1 mark]*, so it stops producing the carbon dioxide that makes the bread rise *[1 mark]*.

Page 84 — Selective Breeding
Q1 The farmer should choose the bean plants that are best at surviving the drought *[1 mark]* and let them reproduce *[1 mark]*. He should then continue this process over several generations *[1 mark]*.

Page 85 — Fish Farming
Q1 E.g. the diet of food pellets is carefully controlled/high quality to maximise the amount of energy the fish get *[1 mark]*. This causes the fish to grow bigger and faster to provide a good source of protein *[1 mark]* / Food is provided regularly *[1 mark]* to make sure that big fish don't eat the smaller ones/to prevent intraspecific predation *[1 mark]*.

Page 86 — Genetic Engineering
Q1 It can improve the yield of the crop *[1 mark]*, because herbicide-resistant crops can be sprayed with herbicides to kill weeds without the crop being damaged *[1 mark]*.

Page 87 — Cloning
Q1 E.g. remove explants from the shoot tips of the tree *[1 mark]*. Sterilize the explants *[1 mark]* and grow them in vitro/place them on a medium containing nutrients and growth hormones *[1 mark]*. Plant the resulting small plants in soil and put them in glasshouses to allow them to grow *[1 mark]*.

Index

Index